WHY

INDEPENDENTS

RARELY

WIN ELECTIONS

And How They Could Become More Competitive

Paul D. Rader

Disclaimer

The views expressed in this book are my own and do not reflect the views of my employers or others.

Why Independents Rarely Win Elections
© Copyright 2021 Paul Rader

For more information, email paulraderwrites@gmail.com.

Print ISBN: 978-0-578-98279-3
eBook ISBN: 979-8-9850853-0-3

Want to learn more about the various aspects of political science? I curated a quick, free guide of informative resources covering voting by officeholders, news, the function of government, public policy, original analyses, and more!

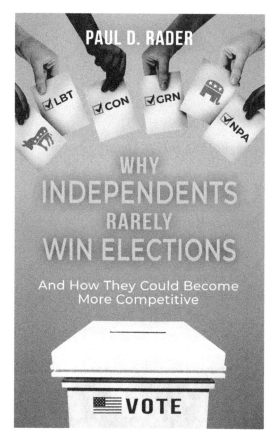

Get a copy by going to the following webpage:

https://bit.ly/wirweguide

Grab your free stuff today!

Contents

Acknowledgments

There are a lot of people who had some impact on me—small and large, direct and indirect, long-term and short-term—that led to the making of this book, too many to name. Though most of them did not even know that I was writing one, they still had a positive influence on making it happen. These family members, friends, mentors, and colleagues have believed in me even when I have had trouble believing in myself.

First, of course, is my family. My mom, dad, and sister have loved and put up with me all my life, even when I can be a rather challenging sort (which, I imagine, is a lot of the time). They have always been in my corner through thick and thin. Thank you.

A special thanks goes to Dr. Susan MacManus, who is the biggest influence on my career aspirations. I took two classes with her during my college undergraduate days at the University of South Florida. (Go Bulls!) Beyond her mentorship, Dr. MacManus has also vouched for me on multiple occasions, including job opportunities and applying to graduate school at the University of Florida. (Go Gators!) I would not be where I am today without her teaching, help, and friendship.

Authors don't ever get books released without the help of others in the process. Thus, I also want to give a shout-out to my editor Carly Catt, my coach Kerk Murray, my formatters at Cutting Edge Studio, and Self-Publishing School for having the most direct impact on making this book happen. This whole process of writing my first book has been an incredible learning experience, and there was a considerable amount of work completed that I couldn't possibly have done on my own.

Thank you to the faculty in, or affiliated with, my graduate school program at the University of Florida who taught me. Their instruction opened my eyes to just how much there is to know about political science and exponentially increased my own understanding of it. And thank you specifically to Dr. Beth Rosenson, who took the time to write the foreword for this book.

The faculty were not the only people at the University of Florida that deserve credit. I had some great classmates, and we all helped each other out considerably in completing coursework and studying the content we learned—some of which informed my writing in this book. As we were told when we were there, we'd all have to lean on each other.

My gratitude also goes to my former and present colleagues who threw their support behind me for writing this book. They gave me encouragement and confidence to continue pursuing this opportunity. Much of the professional work I have undertaken, thanks to opportunities from my employers, imparted a lot of knowledge that was crucial to this book.

And finally, thanks to you, the reader. You can't write books if there is no audience for them, after all. This is my first book, and hopefully not the only one. It means a lot that you would take the time to read what I have to say.

Foreword

Paul Rader's timely and informative book addresses the question of why independent candidates have such a hard time winning elections and how they might become more competitive. Given his academic background (BA in political science and MA in political campaigning) and his real-world experiences working in the campaign world and for several non-partisan organizations such as Ballotpedia, Rader is perfectly situated to shed light on this important topic in American politics.

The book analyzes the difficulties faced by independent candidates through various lenses. For example, it analyzes the impact of individual voter psychology on the fate of independents and the influence campaign committees, pollsters, and the media to understand why the deck is stacked against independents. Most scholars only focus on independents from one vantage point, such as why voters identify as independents or how electoral institutions present major hurdles for independent candidates.

Rader's work, by contrast, draws on and synthesizes multiple aspects of the political landscape in which independents are situated, providing a comprehensive picture of the challenges they face and offering much-needed historical perspective on why it is so challenging for independents to win office. In the process, Rader clears up some common misconceptions about who fits under the label of "independent" and discusses ways that independents might become more viable. This is another difference between this book and other works on independents.

While acknowledging the tough road independents face, Rader is not entirely pessimistic about their chances, and he offers concrete suggestions that can contribute to their success.

Notably, while the book is deeply grounded in classical and current scholarly literature, it is written in a user-friendly, easily digestible manner while at the same time providing analysis that is sophisticated and nuanced. It will be of great interest and appeal to both academics and "regular folks."

I got to know Paul when he was a graduate student at the University of Florida working toward his MA in political campaigning. He was a student in two graduate seminars of mine, on American political institutions and political communications. Paul stood out for his keen analytic ability and his talent at distilling and making sense of large quantities of information. His ability to approach charged political topics with an open mind and a focus on the evidence was also notable, as was his interest in using political science knowledge to inform the general public as well as the rarified world of academia. These qualities are on clear display in this book.

Beth Rosenson
Associate Professor of Political Science, University of Florida

Chapter 1

Why This Book and What Is It About?

In a March 2019 Pew Research Center study, 38% of Americans described themselves as independents.[1] In April 2021, Pew found that only 24% of Americans could trust the government "most of the time" or "just about always."[2] Early in 2021, global analytics and prominent polling firm, Gallup, found 63% of people polled wanted a third political party to seriously challenge the Republican and Democratic Parties—an all-time high in the firm's tracking.[3] Public trust in government is near record lows, and there is widespread dissatisfaction with government, particularly when it comes to Congress.[4] [5] Judging by these statistics and many more, this malaise regarding government can sound like it is ready to shake up the political system as we know it completely.

Despite public opinion, the two-party system is still a never-ending struggle between the Republican and Democratic Parties; they are deeply tied into the country's political fabric. Rarely do we see someone labeled as something other than Republican or Democrat win public office, especially at the federal level. The media attention is constantly on what the two major parties and their members are doing, while coverage of third-party and nonparty candidates is sparse. Overall, voters overwhelmingly still pick candidates from one of the two biggest political parties despite their frustrations with them. The rate of victory for incumbent officeholders' re-elections is still sky-high.

But why?

It is hardly the first paradox regarding the discrepancy between what voters *say* they want and what they *do* about it. For example, we have what we political scientists call "Fenno's Paradox." It is named after the political scientist Richard Fenno who discovered that, despite critically low approval rates of Congress as a whole, we tend to support the particular member of Congress that represents *our district*.[6] It's like the old playground trash-talk that young kids say about each other's fathers, except it's "*My* member of Congress is better than *your* member of Congress!" In US House elections, we can only vote on candidates in the district we live in and not in other districts. (For example, those who reside in Ohio's eleventh congressional district can *only* vote on Ohio's eleventh district candidates). Thus, this seeming contradiction leads to high re-election rates of members of Congress despite most Americans hating the institution itself. If most people are re-electing their district's US House Representative, then Congress is not going to change much, if at all, and the vast majority of people will continue hating Congress.

There's also a divergence between what voters *say* they want and how they *apply* what they believe. Observations of public opinion regarding the role of government in our lives have shown what political scientists call a "symbolically conservative but operationally liberal" mindset. This means that, ideally, we want the government to keep its hands off our day-to-day lives, but in the context of specific programs, we support more government involvement.[7]

A Bit About My Own Journey: How I Came to Tackling These Questions

Why do so many voters pick either Republican or Democrat, even when they are intensely displeased with their parties and, sometimes, the individual candidates? Before graduate school, I had only a little bit of understanding why. For example, I had heard the argument that voting for an independent was a "waste of a vote" plenty of times. However, these past few years—including graduate school, more career experience in political science, and observations and writing on my own time—have shown me that the answer is far more complex than it seems.

The analytical side of politics—the nuts and bolts of why things operate the way they do—is what draws me to the subject. It is certainly *not* directly participating in the conflicts themselves. One of the main goals of my career is to bridge the knowledge gaps that the public has about politics as much as possible from a nonpartisan angle.

But first, that required closing *my own* knowledge gaps— or, more accurately, make progress on closing them. No matter what the subject is or how experienced you are, there is far too much information to learn still, and there always will be. Entering graduate school in 2017 started opening my eyes to just how little I really understood about politics. The academic and practical sides of the program's education tackled political science in ways I never even remotely considered. You will see some of what I learned then in this book, along with what I have gathered on my own.

At the midway point of my grad program, our class had to complete a summer internship that needed to be approved by our program director. I had already decided that I wanted to do nonpartisan, analytical work for a living, which made me apprehensive about doing an internship—even though I knew I would have to do one before I even signed my acceptance letter to the program. There were already plenty of people with their own agenda who refused to acknowledge their own bias, trying to convince people they had all the facts and no opinions and constantly shoving their beliefs down dissenters' throats. I wanted something different. I wanted to have impartial credibility so that I could reach out to a wide range of people.

As I thought over potential options, an opportunity came that my program director passed along: to work with someone affiliated with our program, which assisted independent candidates' campaigns and independent organizations. I had reasons to apply other than apprehension about working with the parties. It was something that I was genuinely curious about. Our studies, both the academic and the practical, already dealt with the Republican and Democratic Parties extensively. Of course, there was still far more to learn about those things, but it is exceptionally rare to get that kind of insight into independent campaigns without truly experiencing it for yourself.

The internship finished around three months later. It taught me a great deal about the inner workings of independent politics: how it strategizes, polls, fundraises, reaches out for support, and so on. Even when I was not directly involved, I would learn from what my coworkers were doing—which was easier in a tiny group like ours instead of a larger organization. Those three months rounded out a lot about my education in a way that working for a partisan group could not provide. While it did not come as a surprise that independent campaigns must fundamentally operate differently than Republican and Democratic campaigns, I did not realize just how much that was the case.

In the second and final year of the program, I sometimes thought about class lessons regarding how they would apply to independent campaigns, even if the material did not directly concern independents. While I had to be careful about extrapolating data and making erroneous assumptions, some of the conclusions I came to concerning independent candidates at least seemed to be logical. I did not "crack the code" by any means, but I started to realize many of the bits and pieces explaining why independents had such a tough time winning elections. As it turns out, there are a lot of bits and pieces.

Looking at the Situation from All Angles

It is regularly accepted that the Republican and Democratic Parties are the dominant forces of politics and that there is no other serious game in town. After all, the vast majority of all things politics runs through them. Many people who participate in politics in some way—and even some of those who abstain from politics completely—probably know that the choices in general elections usually boil down to whether one chooses the "red" or "blue" candidate, even if they do not know much else beyond that.

Much lesser discussed, however, is *why* elections

ultimately end up picking between the two main parties almost every time. The public rarely gets anything more than a cursory glance of this, if even that. There appears to be a hunger for something different, a widespread dissatisfaction with much of American politics. It seems an entirely new power structure should be around the corner, but it inevitably ends more in favor of the Republican Party or the Democratic Party.

It is explored to some extent at the academic level, though the research is relatively scant even then. The focus is much more commonly on the two main parties (which is reasonable, as they are the major players), and the research is often based on the perspectives of those parties. An academic inquiry rarely focuses predominantly on the point of view of what we consider "independents." Even when academic works are not sharply focused on or do not even regard independents, it does not mean that you cannot think about the implications they hold for independents. It does warrant some caution when extrapolating, however.

To the best of my knowledge, there has not been a truly comprehensive dive into what makes it so hard to win as an independent. There have been plenty of studies, news reports, and so on that have focused on smaller aspects, but as far as I know, there has not been a serious attempt at putting it all together and seeing how all these factors work in tandem against independents. That is a major reason why I am writing this book. It does its best to incorporate the academic, the practical, and the theoretical sides to the discussion. Each has its own strengths and can make up for the weaknesses of the other two.

The media also plays a large role in hindering the understanding of independents. They are not often covered in the news. Still, even when they are, the media tends to focus on gaffes, how an independent candidate could "spoil" an election, or whether independent voters will support the Republican or Democratic candidates primarily. The media also largely focuses on entertainment, and what is informative does not always coincide with what is interesting to media consumers. How TV, radio, social media, and so on cover independent politics has a significant influence on how the public perceives independent voters and candidates, including other independents.

What This Book *Is* and *Is Not*

This book is trying to answer the overarching question: Why do independents have such a hard time breaking into political office? While the reasons politics works the way it does have intrigued me in general for a long time, I have had a particular fascination with this topic since I was in graduate school. Not that it had not crossed my mind previously, but my studies both in the classroom and in an applied setting in the last few years have brought it to the forefront of my mind when it comes to politics. Why *do* we say we want someone that is not a Republican or Democrat (usually for president), but we almost never take the actual step of voting for them?

You have probably heard some voters say that voting for an independent, a third-party, etc., would be "wasting a vote" and that they have to vote for the "lesser of two evils." Perhaps you have felt this way as well. Certainly, this belief plays a large role, but it is not just a matter of political efficacy. There is so much more to why we have two dominant parties than this—a plentiful number of nooks and crannies to consider. Many of these more intricate, lesser-known factors are what this book is diving into.

It is also important to note that this is not just about the presidency—or Congress, for that matter. I believe that politics has become far too nationalized, with state and local offices far too often pushed to the side or analyzed in terms of what is going on in national politics. States and localities have much different, though sometimes similar, sets of circumstances that do not make for clean one-to-one comparisons with the federal government. The lower levels of government are too important not to account for, especially since they have the most direct impact on our lives. They also can have different effects on independent politics than higher offices, as independent candidates' campaigns tend to be slightly more successful for more local levels of government than those of a higher level.

Some misconceptions will likely arise from this book that I want to address before they come up if they have not already. This book is *not* a step-by-step guide for third-party and nonparty candidates, and it is not trying to be. It is not meant to imply that knowing all this stuff will get independents more wins in elections. It is impossible to guarantee that due to the nature of the subject anyway, for reasons you will soon learn about.

This book is also *not* trying to make an argument for *or* against having a strong third-party or nonparty contender. It is not concerned with partisan and ideological debates, and I am not trying to insert my own views regarding them. There are endless amounts of that in the media already. Such disputes are only featured when it comes to how they affect the viability of independent candidates. My arguments are mostly focused on structural and process elements, such as how different types of elections or how voter psychology impacts independents' viability.

I do not want to go the way of many pundits and simply tell you, "This is how it is." I am not going to pretend that I have all the answers or that I have covered every potentially related aspect of this issue. I am a firm believer that generating discussion and giving people things to think about is a much more effective route than simply telling them information. It is how most of my graduate (and some of my undergraduate) classes were, and it made a tremendous difference. The goal is to be as unbiased as possible, though inevitably, some will creep in due to the subject matter. I seek to cover as much ground as I can without it getting overly complicated, which politics can quite often be.

Lastly, this will not be a truly comprehensive book of all the roadblocks that face independent candidates for office. That would take far longer than just this one book to fully flesh out. The discussion would have to include a lot of tangential subject matter that, at first glance, may seem like it has nothing to do with independents. It would bog down the discussion and make things unnecessarily complicated when this book is supposed to be more accessible to everyone. It will, however, discuss the most important issues that independents face in their quests to get elected (or, in the case of campaign operatives, what hinders them from getting their candidates elected).

How Does This Book Look at Independents?

The issues for independent campaigns have many facets. Here is a quick preview of each roadblock that will be examined in-depth in the corresponding chapters.

- **Chapter 2: What exactly *is* an independent?** Words

get thrown around with reckless abandon in politics all the time, but their definitions matter. There is some confusion about what an independent exactly is. Addressing independents, in general, requires understanding what makes an independent an independent. There is a tendency to lump them all in one group when independents can vary wildly in the kind of voter they are—and not all of them have the same view of what being an independent means.

- **Chapter 3: Why do we have two parties?** Except for one brief period in the United States' history under the US Constitution, there have always been two political parties that have thoroughly dominated the landscape. It is necessary to understand why the system is so given to this reality and has always been, while it is not the same case for some other countries.

- **Chapter 4: How does voter behavior and psychology hinder independent candidates' chances?** It is not just a matter of "wasting votes." There are many mental mechanisms that stand in the way of third options in elections. There are multiple ways for voters to evaluate elections. A lot of these psychological elements work in ways we do not realize.

- **Chapter 5: How do independent candidates and organizations hamper themselves?** The cards are already stacked against them, but sometimes independents make key mistakes that defeat any remote chance of success. When you are an independent, your margin for error is incredibly small.

- **Chapter 6: How does the rate of independent**

victories differ based on the type of election? Levels of success are not the same for these candidates across the board. They vary by level of government, where the elections are, and other factors affecting the basic circumstances of these elections (e.g., the type of primary being held). While independents have immense difficulty regardless, some types of elections can be more conducive to achieving victory than others.

- **Chapter 7: How do independent campaigns compare to Republican and Democratic ones?** As different as independent campaigns must operate, there are some commonalities in what they need and what the Republican and Democratic Parties need to win elections. Most, if not all, of these, are significantly harder for independents to achieve or do sufficiently than for the major parties.

- **Chapter 8: What other unique elements to independent candidates' campaigns impede their chances of victory?** Some issues are more specific to independent campaigns, such as ballot access problems (i.e., the laws regulating how candidates even get on the ballot in the first place). These things have become ingrained in the political system itself, making them much harder to root out.

- **Chapter 9: How does media, academic, and public attention, or lack thereof, affect independent candidates' chances of winning?** Almost all the interest and attention are toward the Republicans and Democrats, both on and off the campaign trail. How this all happens contributes greatly to why independent candidates often get left on the backburner at the ballot box.

If you are really itching for more independent candidates to win office, or at least make some more noise to threaten the Republican and Democratic Parties, this might make things seem incredibly bleak. But the picture is not totally grim for you. It is just most important to address what the biggest problems are that independent candidates face first. If you see the two-party system's dominance as an issue or a full-blown crisis, you first must understand all the reasons why things are the way they are before you can try to fix the problem. This book will not just leave it at the blockades to independents and be done with it. Considerations of what the strong suits for independents are and what steps to take to change the system are featured in Chapters 10 and 11, respectively. The conclusion will briefly discuss the future of independent campaigns.

With that out of the way, it is time to get into the thick of things. Before the conversation can go anywhere, though, we must ask and answer a seemingly obvious question: Just what exactly is an independent? As you will find out, the answer is quite complex.

Chapter 2

What Is an Independent?

Independents have a problem with the very definition of what an independent is.

The proportion of people who self-identify as independents today was not always so high. Pew Research Center and Gallup polling data indicate that Democrats have almost always outnumbered Republicans, and both parties once dwarfed the number of independents. Yet as the 1960s and 1970s rolled in, there was a noticeable jump in the number of self-identified independents.[8] Possible contributors to this include the unpopularity of the Vietnam War and the Watergate Scandal under President Richard Nixon.

Recent years have seen a rise in the number of self-identified independents. Late January 2021 polling by Gallup resulted in 50% of survey respondents answering in this manner (though the number has fluctuated considerably throughout 2021, with Gallup gauging only 35% of people as self-identified independents in May 2021). According to Gallup historical trends in reported partisan affiliation as of June 2021, independents have been a plurality since December 2012 (i.e., they outnumber either Republicans or Democrats, but not both).[9] Big spikes and drops in percentage points are not uncommon in polling in the short-term, but to be a plurality for nearly a decade straight is noteworthy.

Surely, then, independent political candidates are due for a breakout in the near future, right? No. You do not have to peer beyond the immediate, surface-level statistics much to see why this is a faulty assumption. These citizens may call themselves independent, but what do they mean by it? That was not a question that Gallup poll asked, and most polls do not. Thus, we need to approach the question in other ways.

The Definition of "Independent"

You might be asking yourself why there is an issue here. It might seem like a straightforward concept to some observers. Perhaps you wonder why I would make such a big deal about a clear-cut definition for the term. Some politicians, activists, and regular voters might be comfortable wildly slinging around terms in an insulting manner with little regard to the true definitions of said words. It's like kids or young adults recklessly throwing a football across the field in a pick-up game. They often focus on the flashiness or sensationalism without thinking about the lasting consequences or how detrimental it can be. All that matters to them is that the result is beneficial to them and harmful to the opponent.

In *political science*, however, definitions mean everything. That goes for academia in general. It is one of the most necessary pieces to making a formal academic study to measure something. While this book is not trying to follow that format, it is still just as important to make clear what we mean by certain words. If we are not clear on what these phrases and expressions denote, how can we be on the exact same page about independents throughout this book? I promise it will all make sense why I'm making such a fuss about definitions.

So, what exactly is an independent? What people usually mean seems to be "anyone who is not a member of either the Republican or Democratic Parties." That seems simple enough on the surface, but it is awfully broad even for an umbrella term. Within that sphere is a myriad of other labels that people take. An independent in this sense could be someone who is not affiliated with any party at all, or they could be part of any of the many third parties, such as a Libertarian Party member. To complicate things further, you can find a party actually named the Independent Party, the Independence Party, or both in some states. I've noticed some voters will register with either of those third parties because they are under the impression that that is what being an independent voter is.

What about people who choose not to affiliate with a party at all? That seems to be as independent as one can get. The categorizations might differ between states, but they are almost always called "NPAs" (no party affiliation), "no party preference," or "unaffiliated." In Alaska, there is another classification called "undeclared." An undeclared voter is registered to vote but has not picked any specific label at all—*including* NPA. They are a registered voter, and that is all there is to it. Then you have nineteen states that do not track voter registration by party at all.[10] [11]

The staggering number of different labels a voter can take that are not Republican or Democrat shows how a nebulous definition of what an independent is can be problematic. Not every independent identifies in the same way. Some third-party voters may opt to predominantly call themselves members of their third party instead of simply an "independent." With how broad the umbrella term is, you cannot look at each subgroup within it the same way all the time. For example, the Constitution Party often differs greatly from the Green Party, and both will not necessarily be the same as a nonparty independent.

"But Are You *Really* an Independent?"

Oftentimes in polling, when a respondent says they are an independent, pollsters will press just a little bit further by asking what party they normally *lean* toward. Thus, you get "Republican leaners" and "Democratic leaners." This is significant for several reasons.

- Campaign pollsters can use this information to get a sense of the voters they need to make sure their candidate reels in, lest that leaner decides to just stay home or even vote for a different candidate. If it is a nonpartisan pollster like Gallup or Pew, they may ask that question for whatever research they are trying to conduct.

- Some people do not want to admit they prefer one party or the other, giving them an out to give a more accurate depiction of how they vote. This is an instance of what is called a social desirability bias. People sometimes respond in ways they think are socially acceptable, making people reluctant to admit where their political preferences lie.

- Some studies have indicated that "leaners" more consistently and strongly side with that party than some of the registered partisans that are not hard-core supporters of their party.[12]

- That leaner question does not make clear if they are registered with a third party or no party at all. This might make a big difference in which major party they lean toward—and if you are with a campaign, that difference could mean how likely their vote will truly be up for grabs. Greens are usually more liberal and likely to side with the Democrats. Constitution Party members are usually more conservative and likely to side with the Republican Party. Nonparty voters are more of a wildcard. Since the questions do not probe that deeply into the kind of independent those voters are, it may be harder to gauge how genuine or strong that "leaning" toward a party is.

The Ideology of Independence

Before we go any further, we must clarify that partisanship (i.e., party identification) and ideology are *not* the same, despite how often they are equated or nearly equated in political discussions. (A former professor of mine from graduate school would be beside himself if I did not explicitly make this distinction.) Ideology is one of the most misunderstood political science concepts, even among those whose livelihood is politics. Yes, Republicans tend to be conservative, and Democrats tend to be liberal, and there is plenty of evidence that the party registrants are becoming increasingly uniform on their respective ideologies.[13] [14]

(When somebody is described as a moderate, it means they are ideologically conservative or liberal but not considerably so or are basically in the middle. They may also be described as "somewhat" conservative or liberal.)

Yet, there are varying degrees of conservative and liberal in the respective parties. This is much to the dismay of strictly ideological voters in the parties that bemoan their respective party's "RINOs" and "DINOs." These pejoratives stand for "Republican in Name Only" and "Democrat in Name Only," meaning that they identify as a Republican or Democrat, but do not agree with all or most of their party's core tenets. The partisans that use these terms are most often very ideological and have a strict definition of what a "true" Republican or Democrat is—the American politics version of the "No True Scotsman" fallacy. For these voters, a "true" Republican is strongly and unapologetically conservative; a "true" Democrat is strongly and unapologetically liberal.

If you ask five voters what "conservative" and "liberal" mean, it is quite possible to get considerably different answers from each one. That is because voters do not necessarily share the concept of what being a "conservative" or a "liberal" actually is. Many voters do not think in ideological terms and/or do not know what they mean.[15] [16] [17] For some voters, "conservative" and "liberal" are simply stand-ins for the Republican and Democratic Parties, respectively. Others might think of them in specific issue terms, like pro-life and pro-choice, or more versus less military spending. Some voters might think of them as "more government" and "less government." Then you must consider the fact that one can be conservative on economic issues but liberal on social issues or vice versa.

While this discussion on ideology could go on forever,

we will try to keep it as short and clear-cut as possible. At their *most basic* definitions, a conservative generally wants a more traditional role of government while a liberal generally wants an evolving role. By traditional, we mean policy stances a country's government has customarily supported in its history. What is conservative in one country could be considered liberal in another country and vice versa. In American politics, conservatism means views like a mostly hands-off approach from the government on the economy to let it grow and correct itself to ensure economic freedom, while liberalism means views like government intervention as necessary to help an economy function properly and to ensure equality. Then, there are varying degrees of conservative and liberal therein, with varying levels of agreement (or even disagreement) on typical conservative and liberal tenets.[18]

So, what about the ideology of all these independents? Democrats are generally liberal, and Republicans are generally conservative, but things can get quite murky when we talk about independents. There is a tendency to assume that independents are always in the middle of the political spectrum.

This is not the case, however, and for many independents, it is far from it. Many independents think more like strong partisans in some respects.[19] These independents are called partisan "leaners"—self-identified independents who have said they tend to support one party over the other of the two major parties. Pew data for 2018 had over half of both Republican and Democratic leaners respond that they viewed the party they leaned toward favorably and the opposing party unfavorably, and the share of leaners identifying as either conservative or liberal has increased since 2000.[20]

Other independents might not necessarily think that the parties are extreme, but they have a different set of ideals or different points of emphasis on the same side of the spectrum as the Republican or Democratic Parties. Some independents are just flat-out embarrassed by their party, hiding their true partisan leanings from others and engaging in less political action like voting or volunteering for campaigns.[21]

In any case, good examples of third parties that would not be characterized as centrists are the Constitution and Green Parties. The national website of the Green Party emphasizes values, ideals, and policies that would be mostly considered liberal (left-leaning), such as a very ecology-oriented economy (hence their name "Green Party"), significant scaling-back of military spending, and social justice.[22] [23] The national website of the Constitution Party, on the other hand, espouses values, ideals, and policies that would be mostly considered conservative (right-leaning) such as original intent of the Constitution (hence their name "Constitution Party"), pro-life views, and emphasis on states' rights.[24] [25]

How Should We Look at Independents?

Independents, then, come from all over the political spectrum. Some of them are closer to the middle, concerned about the Republican and Democratic Parties pulling too far to their respective sides, but there are still plenty of them that go further to the right or the left than the two major parties. Some independents fall within the "normal" ideological bounds of the Republican and Democratic contingents but still register as a third party or no party at all. That can be because of all sorts of reasons.

- They simply do not want to admit that they are most suited toward one party and want to see themselves as something less mainstream. This could indicate a social desirability bias, a phenomenon (particularly in polling) where a respondent chooses what they feel is a socially acceptable answer to a question. While there are vocal partisans and ideologues, the frustration many people feel with the intense political divide makes some voters feel a stigma toward being too attached to one side.

- Like many voters, they do not think much if at all about ideologies, or they are unsure about where the parties' ideologies exactly lie, and they feel it is best to not pick one party or the other. Depending on how closely you pay attention to politics, one might think, "How could someone not know what a party stands for?" Always remember that not everyone pays the same degree of attention to the regular goings-on of the government and campaigns.

- They are more so retrospective voters who reward or punish the party in power with their votes based on how well they (the voters) are doing personally, usually economically. Whether the party in power is truly responsible or not is beside the point; it is a matter of how these retrospective voters perceive things.

The confusion that arises from defining independents suggests that the problem is not just these voters' "fault"; it is complicated. What if we just do not fully understand what independence really is? You could argue we have been looking at it the wrong way. We have been imposing our own views on what an independent is or should be. Does an independent have to be a centrist? Are they just closet partisans trying to hide? Do they just not know what platforms the major parties typically espouse or even their personal beliefs?

For some independents, party identification is meaningless. There is a big difference between asking whether someone prefers a party and whether they are independent. The term "independent" might not even mean anything to them.[26] After all, third parties often get thrown under the "independent" umbrella, even though you cannot describe them as having no party preference. You might be able to say they have no *major* party preference (i.e., Republican or Democratic).

There may also be a subtle but critical difference regarding people's attentiveness toward politics in general. Responding with "no party preference" might indicate a subtle but critical difference regarding the respondent's awareness of politics. The typical polling question is, "Generally speaking, do you consider yourself a Democrat, a Republican, an independent, or something else?" That last option could lead to all sorts of different choices. Someone who is totally apathetic about politics may simply choose "Independent." Yet if there is an option to say, "no party preference," that respondent may signal that they are "somewhat aware of political matters but lack responsiveness to the concepts of either partisanship or independence."[27] "True" independents, ones who definitively have no preference, tend to avoid politics completely.[28]

A Republican or Democrat in an Independent's Clothing?

You might also occasionally see a candidate running as an

independent who would otherwise call themselves a Republican or Democrat and normally appear in their respective party's primary election. The candidate sees no path to victory running in a primary and tries to circumvent the issue by simply running as an independent. In many elections, third-party and/or nonparty candidates do not have a primary election and, subsequently, go straight to the general election. So, the would-be Republican or Democrat running as an independent tries to guarantee themselves a shot at winning the office.

Similarly, you may also find a candidate that *did* run in a primary election, lost, and then filed to run in the same election as an independent. Not every election legally allows for this. It partly depends on filing deadlines to appear as a candidate on the ballot—independents may have a different date than Republicans or Democrats do. To stop candidates from doing this, some states employ what are called "sore loser" laws. These restrictions state that a candidate who runs for and fails to secure a nomination in a party's primary is prevented from running as an independent in the same election. As of 2014, the only states that did not have any form of a sore loser law were Connecticut, Iowa, and New York.[29]

As usual with politics, there is an even seedier side to this. The Republican or Democratic Parties may be directly involved with the independent candidate—but not to help them win. One party may plant a third candidate to thwart the opposition party from winning. One way this is done is by finding a candidate with at least the same last name as the opposition party's nominee and paying them to stand as a candidate for election. The planted candidate may run just enough ads (typically the pieces of mail from political groups you might get bombarded with near election time) to get enough voters to know about them and be confused by the last name. It is, of course, illegal in most, if not all, cases to engage in such tactics, but legality issues clearly have not stopped many politicians from taking part in such actions before.

How Many People are "True" Independents?

How many "true" independents are there, then? How much has the electorate truly polarized? That depends on who you ask and how they interpret data, along with how we even define an independent. Since "true" independents are usually thought of as just centrists/moderates left behind by the Republican and Democratic Parties, we will treat them as such in this section for simplicity. How many people there really are in the middle of the political spectrum has enormous implications for these kinds of independents.

Conveniently, some scholars and general political observers have documented debates about this topic, though they do not specifically refer to independents. While it is an oversimplification, there are generally two sides to the issue that scholars and observers tend to gravitate toward: (1) those who believe that voters in the "middle" are disappearing, and/or there is a rather small proportion of middle-grounders, and (2) those who believe that the intense division between voters is overblown and that there is a significant number of Americans who really are not so polarized. Exhibit A comes from the back and forth between longtime scholars Morris Fiorina and Alan Abramowitz.

Abramowitz places himself firmly in the camp of the disappearing middle ground. In his book, *The Polarized*

Public?, he argues that polarization has been continually climbing since the mid-1900s and that there is a serious chasm between the Republican and Democratic Parties based on racial, ideological, cultural, and geographic lines.[30] For him, polarization energizes a large proportion of the public, not just the elites (i.e., those involved in politics for a living, such as officeholders), and it turns out voters.[31] This polarization has also contributed to a decline in the competitiveness of US House elections.[32] Many of these races have become so predictable in which major party wins that the party with no chance will often not even bother to run a candidate or will put a bare minimum effort behind them.

Fiorina, on the other hand, is much more skeptical. He points to self-identification polling, where the number of independents has shot up since the mid-1960s, and self-described moderates have almost always been the plurality over conservative and liberal since the 1970s.[33] Gallup and Pew Research Center data more recent than that particular study of Fiorina's appears to mostly agree on the point on self-identified independents.[34] [35] [36] Gallup also seems to agree somewhat on the point of self-identified moderates in recent years, though self-identified conservatives have slightly outnumbered them according to their research.[37] Since "independent" is more of a partisan indicator and "moderate" is more of an ideological indicator, these are both important figures when discussing how many "centrist independents" there really are. Remember that partisanship and ideology are *not* the same thing, even though they are related. You can identify as an independent while also identifying as something other than moderate.

While he does not totally dismiss the occurrence of polarization, Fiorina instead argues that most of the polarization is being mislabeled, and what is really happening is partisan *sorting*. This means that the parties are becoming more homogenous ideologically—that Republicans have been increasingly identifying as conservatives, and Democrats have been increasingly identifying as liberals. But it does not mean the *whole* electorate is spreading out to polar opposites.[38] Partisanship and ideology are not exactly the same, but they are correlated. Fiorina, as well as fellow political scientists Samuel Abrams and Jeremy Pope, argue that there is not considerably more polarization than fifty years ago in the public.[39]

Which of these camps is right? That is for you to decide, but they both bring up good points. Still, it can make polarization seem greater than it really is if the choices are always extreme. Maybe it is as the seminal V. O. Key Jr. once said, "If the voters can choose only from rascals, they are certain to pick a rascal."[40] Perhaps there are more "true" independents than some political observers think, then. They just need someone to "wake them up."

Summary

Think about all this the next time you see poll results that indicate a high percentage of people open to an independent candidate. If independent voters have wildly varying reasons for calling themselves independents, then there are also wildly varying reasons that they would vote for an independent candidate. Maybe they want someone who is moderate and eschews ideological extremism or, conversely, someone who is willing to go further ideologically than the Republican or Democratic Parties. Maybe these voters do not know about the independent candidates, or they do not think they are good candidates. Maybe they are just retrospective voters picking one of the major parties based on how they perceive the performance of the party in power. Maybe they just do not care at all about politics. It could be for all sorts of reasons.

Whatever the case may be, it causes some confusion if we are not all on the same page on what an independent is. Therefore, we will establish guidelines for this book to cut down on misunderstanding. Unless explicitly stated otherwise, just the word "independent" by itself is a catch-all term defined as *any candidate who neither registers with nor considers themselves a member of the Republican or Democratic Parties.* Thus, it can refer to third party or nonparty. A "centrist independent" more specifically refers to the typical concept of independents as moderates on issues and/or ideology. (I will sometimes also call this a "true" independent.) The terms "third party" and "nonparty" are straightforward.

Now that we have that out of the way, there is something else we must address before getting deep into the matter of why independent candidates have so much difficulty winning elections. Why do we even have two major parties? As you will see in the next chapter, the structure of the political system has been mostly geared toward this reality for almost the entire history of the United States.

Chapter 3

Why We Have a Two-Party System

Independents have a problem with the United States' two-party system.

Here is an exceptionally brief history of the United States' two-party politics. While American politics has not always been Republican versus Democrat, it has been a two-party system for almost the entirety of its existence under the US Constitution. While the Founding Fathers may not have had political parties in mind, they were made soon after the Constitution's ratification, and the Founding Fathers gravitated to them quickly. Parties were necessary to efficiently govern, be organized, and enact their issue priorities.

The Federalist Party counted among its members those who supported the US Constitution's replacement of the Articles of Confederation, the original governing document of the country. The Anti-Federalists, who believed the US Constitution was an overreach of centralized government, would soon form the Democratic-Republican Party (sometimes just called the Republicans). Initially, under the Constitution, the Federalists were clearly the more successful party at the federal level.[41] John Adams became the second president of the United States.

Yet Adams' loss in his re-election effort to Republican Thomas Jefferson in the 1800 election signaled the beginning of the end for the Federalist Party. Federalist control of Congress and the White House was broken. Scandals and blunders ensued in the next couple of decades for the party. They were no longer a credible threat to win elections at the national level, and by the mid-1820s, Federalists faded away from the local level.[42]

This became the one point in US history where it was a one-party system. The Jeffersonian Republicans (supporters of Thomas Jefferson) were the only game in town, but they would undergo an immense transformation in the absence of major opposition. Andrew Jackson, the seventh president of the United States, would seize the reins of the party, reshaping it in his image and changing their name to the Democratic Party.[43]

The rise to power of Jackson led to the formation of the Whig Party, a ragtag collection of political elements united on one basic thing: opposition to Andrew Jackson. After Jackson left office, the Whigs managed to win the presidency twice. But almost as if an omen of things to come, they were two of the shortest presidencies in the country's history. William Henry Harrison set the record by dying a month into office, while Zachary Taylor died less than a year into his own tenure. The Whigs, who counted membership from the North, South, and the burgeoning West, soon started to crumble. With nothing left to unify them after Jackson, the party's continued existence was easy pickings for the hottest political issues of the time—especially the largest stain on the nation's history: slavery.[44]

As slavery and other issues ended the Whigs, the Republican Party of today quickly rose in its place in the 1850s. It absorbed into its ranks former Whigs, Democrats who defected from their party, and the short-lived Free-Soil and "Know-Nothing" Parties.[45] Since then, it has been the Republican and Democratic Parties relentlessly battling it out for political supremacy. That is not to say the parties themselves have not changed, though. Over the course of one-and-a-half centuries, both the Republican and Democratic Parties have been dramatically reshaped multiple times through changing demographic makeups and the countless key issues that have emerged since.

The Third Parties That Have Come and Gone

Despite the system's penchant for two main parties, American history is littered with third parties just like today, though many of them are long gone. Rarely have they ever become a serious threat to the Republican and Democratic Parties. They may have made a huge splash in one election only to go out with a whimper in the next election, if at all. Ten third parties from the 1832 to 1992 presidential elections—the Anti-Mason, Free Soil, Whig-American, Southern Democrats, Constitutional Union, Populist, Progressive/Bull Moose, Socialist, Progressive (not the same as the Bull Moose iteration), and American Independent Parties—all failed to capture at least five percent of the vote or endorse a major party candidate after their breakout campaigns. Sometimes they did nothing at all or simply ceased to exist.[46]

While there are far too many examples to go over, here are some of the most significant examples in national politics. A couple of these were mentioned above.

- The secretive "Know-Nothings" enjoyed a brief period of influence, probably most well-known for their fierce nativist stance—intensely opposed to *any* immigrants seeking to make a new life in America. The Irish, predominantly Catholic and the biggest immigrant group at the time as they sought to escape the famines of their homeland, were a favorite target of the Know-Nothings. (The offensive acronym NINA, which stands for "No Irish Need Apply," originated in this time frame.) The short-lived party, much like the Whigs, would splinter due to the issue of slavery.[47]

- The Anti-Masonic Party, capitalizing on the anti-elitist fervor of the day against targets such as the secret society of the Masons, rapidly rose in popularity but just as quickly declined in favorability. After a respectable third-party showing in the 1832 presidential election, they faded away quickly and came to endorse 1936 Whig presidential nominee William Henry Harrison (who easily has the record of shortest US presidency at just one month). They were mostly absorbed into the Whigs, though they did manage to capture two governorships and fifty-three US House seats.[48]

- The "Bull Moose" Progressive Party under former president Theodore Roosevelt is perhaps the most notable third party in US history. After Roosevelt served as president from 1901 to 1909, his protégé

William Taft won the election to succeed him. During Taft's term, Roosevelt became angered at what he felt was an insufficient progressive record by Taft as the nation's chief executive. Thus, Roosevelt threw his hat back into the ring for the 1912 presidential election. He was highly successful in thwarting Taft's re-election prospects, the former garnering an even greater share of the popular vote (27.4%) than the latter, paving the way for Democrat Woodrow Wilson to claim victory.[49] Roosevelt declined the 1916 nomination, and as the progressive movement faded, so did the Bull Moose Party.[50]

The speculation of former president Donald Trump founding his own party and naming it the Patriot Party is far from the first time there was talk or even a potential threat of a third political party becoming a real contender. Both the Democratic and Republican Parties have faced several intense internal conflicts that risked fracturing themselves in two more than once. In a few cases, a faction *did* break from the greater party.

The prime example on the Democratic side would be the schism between Northern and Southern Democrats in the mid-twentieth century. Much of the Southern Democratic group, nicknamed the "Dixiecrats," broke off to form their own party—the States' Rights Democratic Party (SRDP). The gulf between them centered on civil rights for racial minorities, with the SRDP vehemently opposed to policies like desegregation and integrated busing, while avidly advocating Jim Crow laws. Not all Southern Democrats joined the SRDP[51].

A faction of Republicans broke apart from the wider party for the 1872 presidential election and named themselves the Liberal Republican Party. Republican Ulysses S. Grant's administration was rife with corruption prior to civil service reform in the government. The Liberal Republican Party was angry at this and attempted to thwart his election by forming a coalition with the Democrats. This would greatly backfire on the Liberal Republicans as many Democrats refused to endorse the Liberal Republican presidential nominee, Horace Greeley. The Liberal Republican Party quickly ceased to exist following the 1872 election.[52]

But Why the Democratic and Republican Parties in Particular?

Despite all the challenges they have faced, the Republican and Democratic Parties have remained steadfast, avoiding the fates of the Federalist and Whig Parties. They have been the dominant, overarching forces in politics for more than one-and-a-half centuries. The Democratic Party has been around for practically the whole existence of the United States under the US Constitution, while the Republican Party has been around for a couple of decades or so preceding the Civil War.

What makes the Democratic and Republican Parties so durable? Why have they lasted, becoming these political behemoths, while the Federalists and Whigs faded away? Both the Whigs and the Federalists faced an extraordinary set of circumstances.

The Election of 1800 broke Federalist control of both the White House and Congress, and their power continued to dwindle in the years to come.[53] Then the War of 1812 was waged with Britain attempting to bring the United States back into its empire. The pro-Britain economic policy of the

Federalists, and the rise of nationalism from the pivotal Battle of New Orleans, would prove disastrous for the Federalist Party.[54] [55] The limited geographical reach of the Federalists, public perception of them as aristocratic, and secession threats including a plot by Aaron Burr (yes, *that* Aaron Burr) compounded their problems to bring about the end.[56]

The Whigs—already a precarious convergence of sectional interests from the North, South, and burgeoning West—were already having trouble balancing party members' interests, and slavery would prove to be the biggest and final nail in the coffin for the party's existence. The only thing that held them together for so long was their bitter opposition to President Andrew Jackson, who completely reshaped the Jeffersonian Republicans into his own image, earning them the nickname "Jacksonian Democrats."[57] With Jackson gone after two terms, there was nothing to hold the Whig Party together. While their intraparty conflicts were over many issues because of their regional priorities, their intense internal divisions over the biggest issue of the day, slavery, were the lethal blow.

Even with all these crises, however, there still never was a serious third-party contender. The Whigs filled the void left by the Federalists, quickly becoming the second major party. Then the Republican Party rapidly eclipsed the Whig Party. While the Republican and Democratic Parties had never met any cataclysm as the Federalists and Whigs did, that is not the only reason for their continued existence. Political campaigns became ever more sophisticated in reaching out to voters, and the Republicans and Democrats have had the capabilities and know-how to completely ingrain themselves in American politics, which are some other significant contributors to their persistent presence all these years.

What Makes Our System So Conducive to Two Dominant Parties?

Throughout this nation's political history, the system has always been ruled by one of two parties, save for a couple of brief periods of one-party rule. There has never been a serious, long-lasting third option on a widespread scale that could challenge the Democrats and the Republicans alike. Teddy Roosevelt's bid for the 1912 presidential election was arguably the closest, but his Bull Moose Party went nowhere after that (though, his main goal was just to defeat Taft anyway).

Even if Roosevelt had tried to muster another third-party challenge, with himself or somebody else at the helm, a choice outside of the mainstream was never going to last long. Over the course of more than two centuries, the two-party system has remained nearly always stout. Clearly, the system is built for two parties, whether intentionally or not. Why?

Political scientist John Aldrich gives some insight into the situation. Political parties are durable entities, meaning they do not go down easily, and they are embedded in our political system. There are incentives for politicians to be part of a party: they combine groups of people that are vast and diverse, yet similar enough (or at least not directly opposed to each other) in their interests that they can band together to achieve their goals. Forming such alliances gives ambitious politicians access to resources and support in their quest for public office. As a result, parties help their candidates win more often and share in the rewards of election (e.g., receive funding for district projects).[58]

What About Other Countries?

If you have an interest in international politics like I do, or at least casually observe it, you may have noticed that some countries have more than two parties that make serious bids in vying for control by forming majority-rule governments. They must form coalitions because none of the parties have enough members to take a majority of seats on their own. In Europe, such countries include Germany, Italy, and Spain. Elsewhere in the world, Israel has a staggering number of political parties that significantly affect who controls the government.[59] Even in some countries where there are still predominantly two political parties, they often must make coalitions to effectively govern and implement their desired policies, such as Germany.

In the United States, however, it is extraordinarily rare that members of a third party or no party at all have a major effect on who rules the majority in government, especially at the federal level. There is rarely any worry about forming a coalition as Republicans or Democrats almost always have enough to form a majority on their own. (One exception is recent compositions of the Alaska State House, where a few Republicans defected to form a coalition with the Democrats and a few independents after the 2018 and 2020 elections.[60] [61]) Why is that the case here but not in some other countries? Some of the biggest reasons are Duverger's Law, proportional representation systems, and cultural intricacies.

Duverger's Law

The tendency toward a two-party system is driven by a force called Duverger's Law, named after French political scientist Maurice Duverger, the man who first described it. It is the inclination of electoral systems that operate on single-member districts (SMDs) and plurality-rule (i.e., election winners simply need the most votes, not necessarily a majority) to create a two-party system.[62] Empirically, Duverger's Law has occurred repeatedly in both plurality and majority-rule elections.[63]

The United States, at the congressional level, is this kind of system, as are most state legislative elections. Each district in these cases has one seat, and elections are usually decided simply by who has the most votes—occasionally, they might require a majority vote. As Duverger's Law indicates, most of these elections will be a Republican versus a Democrat. Even in multi-member districts (MMDs), politics is still dominated by the Republican and Democratic Parties. Of course, it does not mean that independents, whether third-party or nonparty, can *never* win. They just very sparingly have a considerable effect on governance.

Proportional Representation Systems and Multi-Member Districts

One of the biggest reasons for this, and what separates the United States from many other countries, is that virtually every election in the United States is winner-take-all. When one candidate receives the most votes, they get all the spoils for that seat, and the other candidates get nothing for it. These other countries, on the other hand, tend to employ proportional representation systems. In these, even if you or your party do not win, you do not walk away empty-handed. The number of seats in government is awarded to the parties based on the percentage of the vote they get. Proportional representation with districts is far and away the most common electoral system in the world, especially in Europe.[64]

However, a few parts of the US do use something similar to what you may see in proportional representation systems called MMDs, where districts have more than one elected official representing them. However, there are not many of these types of districts in the US. MMDs are used in ten state houses and two state senates in the United States (Vermont and West Virginia use MMDs for both of their chambers). MMDs range from two to eleven legislators.[65]

Note, however, that the presence of multi-member districts does not inherently mean that it is a proportional representation system. In proportional representation, the number of seats awarded to parties is based on the percentage of the vote their candidates received from voters. For example, say that a district has ten seats available. Party A won 30 percent of the vote, Party B won 30 percent of the vote, and Party C won 40 percent of the vote. That means that Party A won three seats, Party B won three seats, and Party C won four seats. In the MMDs in the United States, however, it is simply the top vote-getters who get the corresponding number of seats (e.g., if there are three seats, the candidates with the three highest numbers of votes each get one seat).

Since there are so relatively few MMDs in the US, it is too small a sample size to draw solid conclusions from, but we can still approach it theoretically. Independents might have a somewhat easier time winning a seat in an MMD than an SMD. They may have more chances at winning simply because there are more seats, though this also depends on how many Democrats and/or Republicans are running in that district and how many seats are up in the district. If too many candidates of one party run in a given district, it might split their votes enough that the other party or independent candidates have a shot at winning. Sometimes, a state or county party will urge its own members to withdraw from that district's election to lessen the chance of this happening. Regarding the number of seats, there could be a big difference in chances of winning if it is, say, a district with two seats versus a district with three seats.

Summary

The two-party system has been a bedrock of American politics since just about the country's inception as a free nation. It has taken on a few different forms over the course of the nation's history, but since the mid-nineteenth century, the Democratic and Republican Parties have been stalwarts of governance. While some third parties have made headlines here and there, sometimes even making substantial inroads in Congress and capturing a surprising proportion of the presidential election's popular vote, just about all of them have quickly died out. The third parties that exist now have relatively little influence.

The nature of the US political system, such as through Duverger's Law, has ensured that the system fundamentally stays thoroughly dominated by two political parties. It is not all about the structural conditions of politics, however. As we will learn in the next chapter, we find another significant reason in how politics is perceived by the voters—the very people who make the ultimate decision on who occupies elected offices.

Chapter 4

How Voter Psychology Hinders Independent Candidates

Independent candidates have a problem with voter behavior. Meet John. John is just an ordinary guy, trying to live life while raising a few kids with his wife, Jane. Both John and Jane work full-time. Other developments in life have also kept them busy. They try to listen to politics as much as possible, but they are so frustrated by what they see and hear that it is hard for them to keep paying attention. Still, they feel that it is their duty to keep informed and cast a vote come Election Day, so they try hard to be up-to-date despite their hectic lives.

Suddenly, Election Day is just around the corner. As tired as John and Jane are from work all day, other life problems, and kids who want to play all night, they want to sit on the couch together and watch some TV, but the impending election leads them to try to look up whatever they can about the candidates. They look up their candidates in sources like the Supervisor of Elections website and Ballotpedia's sample ballot tool. In their research, they find that there is an NPA (nonparty affiliated) candidate running in their local state legislative race.

John and Jane have long been looking for an independent candidate to get behind, but they find out that it is considerably difficult to locate information on this contender. When they watched and listened to the news, they have heard nothing about this candidate, only about the Republican and Democrat. Even their local newspaper barely acknowledges that this independent candidate exists. Upon thinking some more, they feel they cannot take a chance on this independent whom they know next to nothing about. If there is more to that candidate that can be found, John and Jane sure do not know where. As a result, they begrudgingly vote for the candidate from the party they usually align with.

Does this story sound familiar? Does it basically describe your experiences? While the exact details are obviously going to differ between people, it is a common tale. When you peer just beneath the surface, you will see that John and Jane's basic psychological processes and behavior are very natural to human beings.

The Costs and Risks of Voting

People are often risk-averse. We tend to place greater value on losses than gains even when the chance of a gain or loss is the same or when the gain is a greater value and more likely. Consider this: If you were to wager $10 for a 70 percent chance to win $50 but have a 30 percent chance to walk away with nothing, many people would not even attempt the wager once. Though the person making the wager will likely end up with more money than when they started, even if they had to make the wager two or three times, the thought of losing the $10 weighs more heavily for some people (especially if they can potentially lose that money two or three times). They think, "What if I lose $20 or $30?"

But costs and risks do not need to be monetary. We often view doing something big and brand new as a giant risk, such as skydiving. The potential rewards are an exhilarating experience, bragging rights, an interesting story to tell, possibly raising money for charity in certain cases, conquering acrophobia, and more. Yet many people will have that pervasive thought of "What if my parachute doesn't open?" Falling a great distance may be far too fear-inducing for someone, possibly even increasing their heart rate or blood pressure to unsafe levels depending on who they are. It is mostly a matter of perception: if we perceive the rewards as worth going for and likely enough to receive, we may accept the risks. Additionally, our emotional state and/or being confronted by a higher chance of loss can also influence us to be more risk-seeking.[66]

Such evaluations of costs and risk-taking help explain a lot about how people vote.[67] Incumbency is a perfect example. Why are there such high re-election rates when it can seem like everybody hates politicians, especially Congress? Enter risk-aversion psychology. Even if you are not enthused about the incumbent or do not know much about them, there is a familiarity and certainty about what you will get as a voter by virtue of the candidate already holding that office. Hence, risk-averse individuals may be less willing to go against that incumbent.[68]

Cost and risk-taking analysis are especially applicable in the case of independent candidates. Think about voters who say that voting for an independent is a waste, even if they detest both the Republican and Democratic candidates. Perhaps you have felt this way as well. On a psychological level, this kind of voter believes the cost and risk of voting for the independent candidate—one whose policies or personality they probably know relatively little about—is too great to let a potential "greater of two evils" win the election. Even if they do not consciously think in terms of cost, risk, or reward, they often will not take the "risk" of voting for a third option.

Also, it is almost always easier to get someone to say no than to say yes. State constitutional amendments that are put in front of voters are a great example of this. If you are opposed to an amendment, you just have to sow enough doubt in voters to get them to feel it is too risky to vote yes. Meanwhile, getting a yes out of people takes a lot of convincing of someone that is not necessarily predisposed to supporting that amendment.

Trying to persuade people to vote for an independent can be much the same way. Most people are not predisposed to vote for someone that is neither a Republican nor Democrat, so it is much easier to sow doubt about voting for an independent. Disgruntled voters from either major party may threaten to vote independent, but the Republican and Democratic Parties' campaigns can often persuade them to stick with the party. Usually, the basic party pitch is something like this: "I know we have our differences within this party, but it is more important that we be unified. After all, you do not want those bad guys on the *other* side to win, do you?"

The Prisoner's Dilemma

If you are an independent candidate trying to convince those disgruntled Democrats and Republicans to throw their support behind you, the problem can also be effectively illustrated by the Prisoner's Dilemma. This is a thought exercise commonly used in economics but can be applied to various disciplines. In the original Prisoner's Dilemma, two suspects are being questioned about committing the same crime. Both are being held in separate rooms, so they cannot know what the other is thinking or saying.

Investigators do not have enough evidence to convict either of them on a greater charge but do have enough to charge them with a lesser crime. Thus, they offer both suspects a chance to rat out the other person about the greater crime in exchange for their own freedom. Since they are already guilty of a lesser crime, both suspects staying silent would limit the amount of prison time to a minimum. This is the best-case scenario. However, the tantalizing prospect of total exoneration may get the prisoners to spill the beans on each other. If they both do so, it leads to them both getting more prison time than if they cooperated. Therefore, the suspects must gauge what they think the other will do. Will the other stay silent in solidarity, or is the chance at freedom too tempting?

Following is a visual of this dilemma for the prisoners. The numbers do not necessarily have to be the ones below; they are just there to make it a clearer explanation.

Length of sentence	Suspect B stays silent	Suspect B betrays A
Suspect A stays silent	A gets a 2-year sentence. B gets a 2-year sentence.	A gets a 10-year sentence. B goes free.
Suspect A betrays B	A goes free. B gets a 10-year sentence.	A gets an 8-year sentence. B gets an 8-year sentence.

Now let us apply it to the context of voting for an independent. You are the independent candidate. Voters A and B are both upset with the party they normally lean toward and are thinking about going with the independent this time. You must convince Voters A and B that they would both benefit the most if they cooperated for a common goal of electing you, instead of picking their party that they may be disgruntled with but consistently choose anyway.

The problem: there is also an incentive for Voters A and B to pursue their own interests or "safe" options—that is, make sure the opposing party's candidate does not win by voting their own. They do not know for sure what the other voter is thinking. They might both want to cooperate by voting an independent but wonder if the other person is looking to be "selfish." If they evaluate that it is too risky to cooperate, they will both pursue their own interests to not be taken advantage of. The result is the least beneficial scenario for both Voters A and B, even though cooperating would have been significantly more favorable to both (from an independent's point of view).

To make it a clearer illustration, we will say Voter A is a Republican and Voter B is a Democrat.

Winner of the election	Voter B votes IND	Voter B sticks with DEM
Voter A votes IND	IND wins or at least has a greater chance.	A "wastes" their vote. B selects the "lesser evil" winner.
Voter A sticks with REP	A selects the "lesser evil" winner. B "wastes" their vote.	Status quo continues as the "evils" duke it out to the end. IND loses.

The "most beneficial" scenario to both sides might be to cast a ballot for the independent in the hopes of victory, but what if the other side chooses to stick with their party's candidate? Now expand the number of participants in the dilemma to whole blocs of voters that might want an independent but are concerned that there are just too many people on the opposing side that will stay put with their party's candidate. In their minds, it is too risky to vote for an independent if the "greatest evil"—the other party's candidate—wins the election. Thus, both party's disgruntled voters will often just "suck it up" and stay with their party's candidate.

While this is somewhat of an oversimplification, this is basically what occurs in the minds of would-be independent voters. They do not necessarily consciously think in the described terms, but when somebody says they fear "wasting a vote," the Prisoner's Dilemma has taken place. If they thought there was much less of a chance of the "greatest evil" winning the election, voters might be more willing to cooperate toward what they would normally view as the best-case scenario: electing an independent.

The Strength of the Party Label

Party identification (party ID, for short) is one of if not *the* most powerful indicator of the way someone is going to vote and view politics, especially if they strongly identify with that label.[69] [70] [71] A lot of voters believe strongly in "voting blue no matter who" and "voting red until I'm dead," and they will not even consider voting for the opposing party, or even outside of their own party at all. They might even hate their own party, but their hate for the opposition is so much greater that they will be damned if the "enemy" wins.

The tug of the party label, however, is stronger on some than on others. In political science, we sometimes refer to members of the Republican and Democratic Parties as "weak" partisans and "strong" partisans. These terms are simply indicators of how strongly these individuals identify with their party. Generally, the "stronger" a partisan is, the more being a Republican or Democrat is a core part of their identity, and the more consistent their beliefs and actions are with their party's beliefs.[72] [73] It is the "weak" partisans that would usually be more likely to vote for an independent, as the pull of the party label is less powerful on them. That still does not mean they actually *will* vote for an independent, as demonstrated in the Prisoner's Dilemma example and the reasons throughout this book.

Symbolism and Heuristics

"Heuristics" is a fancy word for a mental shortcut to reach a solution of some sort. For example, you have probably heard the phrase "righty tight-y, lefty loose-y" when using a screwdriver or drill. You might keep certain restaurants in your head by whether they are Chinese, Italian, Mexican, etc. These are easy ways to remember something instead of having to relearn it repeatedly. Everyone naturally wants to simplify complicated things they do not understand or have much knowledge about, or even when it is something they are familiar with. It makes information easier to digest and remember.

These heuristics are extremely common in politics, and every single voter uses them. Even the most knowledgeable people about politics must employ them. There is too much political information to keep in our memory at any given time, not to mention the rest of the information that life throws at us—all of this competing for attention at once. Heuristics are not necessarily "correctly used," though, and partially depend on how informed voters are about politics.[74] Which heuristics and cues voters use depends on other characteristics such as the voter's awareness of political differences, their interest in politics, and how much they buy into partisan stereotypes.[75][76][77]

(By "correct," we mean that a voter uses heuristics in a manner where they properly apply to the candidates, and that the voter rightly sees a candidate as supporting their beliefs. For example, if you are pro-choice or pro-life, and you use that heuristic to vote for the candidate that supports your side, you have employed the heuristic "correctly." If you mistakenly placed a pro-choice or pro-life label on a candidate with the opposite belief and voted for them because of it, you used the heuristic "incorrectly.")

Many of these shortcuts exist outside of any particular campaign, while others are developed over the course of a single race. Heuristics are an incredibly useful tool to help people keep track of their choices—but they have also been highly detrimental to the political climate when misused or distorted. Key words can be twisted for a politician or party's purposes, thrown about with reckless abandon just to energize their voter base. Examples include the Republican over-usage of the term "socialism" and the Democratic over-usage of the term "fascism," both when referring to the opposing party. Regardless of the words' true meanings, their specters are enough to scare people into taking action against the opposing party.

Heuristics are a good example of just how powerful symbolism can be, for better and for worse. Symbolism can take the form of a well-known figure (e.g., Donald Trump), a set of values (e.g., "traditional family values"), issue stances (e.g., Second Amendment)—you name it. Symbolism naturally resonates with us as human beings. There is a part of us all that desires, even needs, to have something or someone to believe in. Even in cases where the political symbolism is erroneous, they serve their purpose: to galvanize the base of voter support. Symbolism has become so charged that both sides are convinced that the other is evil and immoral simply for espousing contrary views or emphasizing different values.

The symbolism for independents is not even remotely as powerful nor as numerous. After all, a whole chapter of this book showed how divergent people's views can be about what an independent is. There are unclear sets of values to attribute to most independent candidates and few well-known key people to look up to. Despite public opinion about the parties, a candidate setting themselves apart from the parties generally does not affect voter choice. Voters may say they hate the parties, but when an independent candidate reaches out to them to say how different their candidacy is, those same voters still tend to stick with one party. If it were enough to just be outside the system, independent candidates would see much greater levels of support at the ballot box.

The Republican and Democrat Labels

Think about the words "Republican" and "Democrat." Regardless of your political views, what comes to mind when you hear those labels? "Republican" might mean conservative, pro-life, less gun control, a supporter of Trump, higher military spending, and/or a myriad of other things. "Democrat" might mean liberal, pro-choice, more gun control, opposition to Trump, higher domestic spending, and/or countless other things.

You will find some exceptions, of course, but oftentimes, these labels are true, and there has been a trend of increasing unity on various issues within the parties, their ideological makeup, and perceptions of the opposing party.[78] [79] [80] Remember that partisanship and ideology are not on a one-to-one scale. There are some liberal Republicans and some conservative Democrats. Even so, these heuristics are reliable in most cases. Hearing the two major parties' names gives you a general sense of what that candidate is about, even if some specifics are different.

The Independent Label

Now, what comes to mind when you hear the word "independent"?

It is understandable if you must spend more time thinking about heuristics here. A whole chapter of this book was devoted to why the definition of an independent is so tough to pin down. You might come up with something general like "neither major party," but it is tricky to develop general descriptions and reliable mental shortcuts that are more specific. That heuristic might be enough for some voters, but for many others, there will need to be something more persuasive.

- "Centrist?" Some independents are in a third party that is more liberal than the average Democrat or more conservative than the average Republican. Even nonparty candidates might fit that bill.

- "Takes X stance on Y issue?" There are few, if any, unified issue stances across the greater independent political world of the US, so you cannot dependably use any of those either. You might be able to do so with a *specific third party*, but you cannot necessarily apply it to any other third party, and you definitely cannot easily apply it to a nonparty candidate.

- "An ally or associate of a specific politician?" The two major parties have plenty of them that are consistently in the news. Meanwhile, independents have nobody to collectively point to, at least not someone who is well-known.

- "Endorsed by a party or a certain interest group?" There are plenty of these doled out for Republicans and Democrats alike, and some of the heavyweights are routinely touted by a party nominee. However, there are relatively few interest groups that regularly back independents—and even if they do, they rarely hold any weight in the minds of the general voting population.

Even when heuristics are not accurate for some *individual* candidates, most of the existing heuristics we apply to Republicans and Democrats generally are. Republicans and Democrats often tick certain boxes, but there are virtually none to start with for independents. Heuristics are arguably even more critical for independents to get voters to know what they are about. Most Republicans and Democrats make the news more often and have many more resources at their disposal to tell voters what they are about.

Yet someone usually must go out of their way to find information on independent candidates before they can create their own heuristics to remember the candidates by. That can be hard to discover—even for those who are well-versed in political research—or outright impossible. If that is the case, then how can we expect more casual observers to know how to efficiently find the information at all?

Endorsements

Other heuristics often supplement that of party identification. Endorsements are another major example. Campaigns routinely tout announcements of endorsements by well-known party personalities. Republican examples might include Donald Trump, Mitch McConnell, Lindsey Graham, Tom Cotton, Florida Governor Ron DeSantis, and South Dakota Governor Kristi Noem. Democratic examples might include Joe Biden, Barack Obama, Bill and Hillary Clinton, Chuck Schumer, Nancy Pelosi, and California Governor Gavin Newsom. Even when they do not receive these endorsements, candidates often voice their support for these figures to show they are a "true" Republican or Democrat.

It's basically the same case for endorsements by interest groups. Card-carrying members of these organizations, as well as some partisan voters in general, look to these groups' leadership for opinions. The Republican candidate likely is endorsed by groups like the National Rifle Association and Americans for Prosperity. The Democratic candidate likely is endorsed by groups like Planned Parenthood and Run for Something. Some organizations that are nominally nonpartisan still routinely side with one party or the other. For both Republicans and Democrats, interest group endorsements are plentiful, and many of them are well-known.

There are no independent endorsements close to the name recognition that these well-known Republican and Democratic politicians and interest groups get. It is also rare that those partisan groups lend their support to an independent. (This *might* be less often the case in elections where *only* a Republican or *only* a Democrat is running, as the affiliates of the unrepresented party might consider putting their weight behind the independent.) If voters do not know who these independent candidate endorsers are or what they are about, it is unlikely that those voters will pay attention to them or go out of their way to research them. They will be more likely to know about the consistently Republican and Democratic endorsers.

Heuristics and Information Costs

There is always an information cost attached to research. Someone must spend time looking up these candidates, maybe even having to learn *how* to find them, when that person could be doing something else with that time, and there is no guarantee of the "payoff" of finding information. It is likely that this person is going to take a "less risky" approach and vote for the "lesser of two evils" when they have next to no idea how the independent would pan out. Then the voter at least believes they have some idea of what they are going to get; there are plenty of sources that will bombard them with information (real, fake, and everywhere in between) about the Republicans and Democrats. That takes far less time and effort than doing your own research.

Boiling things down to simple, although crude, concepts is effective and limits information costs. Advocacy group mailers, which are those pieces of mail you get from interest groups close to election time, do this a lot. They often list together a small set of the issues they care about most, oversimplify them, and say whether their preferred candidate or the opponent(s) agree or disagree with those issues. It makes for simple cues for that group's supporters to follow, and they do not have to take the extra time to scour for the information themselves.

The Power of Values

The same symbolism and heuristics obviously have varying effects on people; one representation can be agreeable to one group of people while being abhorrent to another. That is because there is something underneath all that symbolism that matters to people at a core level: value systems. Values can also be considered a heuristic when campaigns make a direct appeal to them, but oftentimes, they lie underneath the surface rhetoric. They speak to people on a personal level and help voters relate to a candidate.

Republican values often include things like "family values," "small/limited government," "anti-socialism," and "self-responsibility." Democratic values often include things like "inclusivity," "problem-solving government," "anti-fascism," and "social justice." It is not that the two sides do not share values. They just often place greater emphasis on some values over others, or they see the same values differently. For example, a Republican and/or conservative may see affirmative action as unfair because of intrusive government action and economic freedom restrictions. Meanwhile, a Democrat and/or liberal may see affirmative action as fair because it is a necessary step toward racial equality and that we do not truly have economic freedom for everyone until this true equality is achieved. Which one is right? It depends on what your value systems are and how you perceive them.

Independents certainly have value systems. Everyone does. The issue is that their value systems are harder for voters to pin down, or they have to do a lot of research to find them out. Plenty of people are dissatisfied with the two main parties, but how much do they really value having a candidate be independent of them? Maybe the party they typically support still generally advocates those voters' value systems, or at least appears to.

Then you must account for how independent political views are all over the place. Libertarian Party candidates' values are probably going to be much different than those of Green Party candidates, both of which are likely dissimilar to the values of Constitution Party candidates. Most voters are not going to know what any of those are from the get-go. And what about candidates running as no party at all? If voters do not know what values are most important to an independent candidate or disagree with them enough, then chances are those same voters will not pick that candidate come election time.

The Collective Action Problem

Have you ever tried to get a group of friends together for a fun night out? Was it hard to get everyone onboard for a particular destination or to even respond to the invitation? Maybe you have played an organized sport and know how tough it can be to get everyone on the same page, even on a relatively small team like in basketball.

These examples illustrate the collective action problem. Getting a group, especially a large one, to move in the same direction can be difficult. People in a group must be on the same page with the same goal in mind to be the most effective that group can be. Even Republicans and Democrats, or interest groups affiliated with them, have trouble when trying to turn out their voters. One party leadership position in Congress and state legislatures is called a "whip," a rank dedicated to getting all the party's members, or as many as possible, in unison to support or oppose a bill.

As the economist Mancur Olson discusses in his book on collective action, people do not necessarily act toward their interests. We become more responsive when we have incentives to act in a certain way, but the interest alone is not necessarily sufficient.[81] Regarding the case at hand, there are many voters whose interest may be to elect an independent, but rarely has that been enough reason for them to ultimately choose that option at the ballot box. If it were, independent candidates would win far more often than they do now. Thus, something else must draw those voters into the fold and convince them to vote for an independent.

We can paint a general depiction of what attempts at collective action by independent candidates and campaigners look like. First, independent candidates need to spend a lot more time figuring out who potentially would vote for them. It is rarely, if ever, enough for them to pull from third-party and nonparty voters—either due to being outnumbered, lower turnout rates on the part of independents and moderates, or both—so they must pull moderate Republicans and/or Democrats to their side. Second, independents must reach out to these potential voters in some way and convince them to take a chance on their candidacies.

The major parties are also doing their best to rein back in those moderates as well. They often have the money, the community connections, and the experience to do it, but independents almost never do, at least not to the same extent. Still, it is not always smooth sailing for Republicans and Democrats. Some voters may hold out because they do not find their party's candidate exciting enough, they are outright opposed to that candidate, or they do not see the other candidate as enough of a threat for them to show up to vote. It could be another reason. In the 2016 presidential election, some Republicans threatened to stay home or vote for a third option in protest of Donald Trump; some Democrats made the same threat regarding Hillary Clinton.

If even the Republican and Democratic Parties must expend considerable amounts of resources to get voters to turn out and still sometimes have trouble doing so, then it can be expected that independent candidates and organizations are going to have an even greater slog ahead of them. Furthermore, in politics, it is most often the more organized and well-funded organizations that win out, a fact mostly noted in the context of lobbying.[82] We can apply that to the case of independent candidates as well. They usually have far less organization and far fewer funds to contend with Republicans and Democrats.

Summary

The human mind can be a strange, quirky thing. Countless factors and nuances shape our perceptions and responses to the outside world, many of which we are aware of and many of which we are not. The psychology of voters may be the single biggest stumbling block facing independent candidates for election—how we evaluate whether we should vote for an unknown contestant or the "lesser of two evils," what labels mean to each of us, and how we consider how others may vote. Yet it is one thing to know the underlying mental mechanisms of voter psychology; it is a completely different ballgame when figuring out how to navigate them if you are an independent candidate or campaign operative.

The perceptions of independent candidates do not entirely start with the voters, however. Obviously, there must be independent candidates and apparatuses to perceive in the first place. Voters' reactions depend partially on how those independent candidates and their affiliates try to appeal to voters in the first place. Sometimes, these independents commit errors in their campaign approaches and ruin, or at least severely limit, their chances at winning elections. This is where our next chapter takes us.

Chapter 5

Independent Candidates and Organizations

Independents' problems are oftentimes the candidates themselves or the organizations helping them.

Many candidates have run in elections outside the Republican and Democratic Parties, but exceedingly few are memorable. Rarely do they come close to victory, let alone achieve it. This is especially the case with presidential candidates. Yet there are a few noteworthy cases of a third option making some noise at the ballot box. Perhaps the poster child of independent presidential contenders is the quirky business magnate from Texas in the 1992 election cycle: Ross Perot.

In the 1992 election, Perot garnered nearly twenty million votes, a staggering number for a third option, but he did not capture a single Electoral College vote. His popular vote total was spread so thin that he did not even come close to winning a state.[83] Perot would run again in the 1996 campaign cycle under the Reform Party label, though the novelty had apparently worn off as he only captured roughly eight million popular votes and still could not make any breakthroughs in the Electoral College.[84]

Another man, however, arguably wears the crown when it comes to independent performances in presidential elections, and he was previously president himself: Theodore "Teddy" Roosevelt. Perhaps one of the most well-known presidents that have long since passed on, Roosevelt occupied the office from 1901 to 1909, taking over for William McKinley after he was assassinated shortly into his second term. Toward the end of his tenure, he groomed his protégé William H. Taft to carry on the Republican progressive mantle. (While the original progressives of the late nineteenth and early twentieth centuries share some similarities to the progressives of today, there are also some considerable differences, as the hot button issues of then and now greatly differ.)

Taft's term as president, however, did not pass Roosevelt's litmus test for progressivism, leading him to throw his hat back into the ring for the 1912 presidential election as the Progressive Party candidate. Roosevelt's popularity and name recognition catapulted him far past Taft in the election results, ending with roughly six hundred thousand more popular votes and the Electoral College votes coming in at eighty-eight to eight.[85] Still, Roosevelt himself still fell short of first place, being a third-party choice. With Roosevelt thwarting Taft's chances at reelection, Democrat Woodrow Wilson easily won the 1912 election.

Perot and Roosevelt are anomalies when it comes to independent campaigns for president. In more recent years, nonparty, Libertarian, or Green candidates sometimes make a few headlines here and there, but the campaigns are quickly forgotten after the campaign dust has settled or even before the election is held. Many voters do not even realize or are only vaguely aware that there are third options that are running until they start casting ballots.

Independents at Other Levels of Government

Congress occasionally gets Senators or Representatives that label themselves as independents, but those are still few and far between, and they often caucus with either the Republican or Democratic Parties. Senators Bernie Sanders of Vermont and Angus King of Maine are both nominally independents, but they caucus with the Democratic Party. You might occasionally see a Republican or Democrat switch to a third party or no party at all when they are in office. Former US House Representative Justin Amash changed his affiliation from Republican to Libertarian while in office and briefly considered running for that party's nomination for president, but ultimately chose to neither do that nor seek re-election to his seat in Congress.

When you start peering beyond the federal government and into the state and local levels, independent candidates become somewhat more successful. They are not numerous by any means, but they have been pivotal in policymaking and even shaping the balance of power in some cases, such as in the ever-relevant example of Alaska. In Alaska's 2018 state house elections, Republicans captured a majority of the seats. In an extraordinary occurrence, however, three Republicans and two independents joined with the Democrats to form a majority coalition, electing a Democrat as House Speaker.[86] Even more remarkably, the parties continued to split power following the 2020 elections even as Republicans retained a numerical majority of the house seats. Still, very few independent state legislators came to hold office. As of July 30, 2021, state legislators that were neither Republicans nor Democrats controlled only sixty-three of 7,383 (less than one percent) total seats in the country.[87]

For governorships, there is one recent instance where an independent won an election—once again, Alaska. In the 2014 election cycle, longtime Republican-turned-independent candidate Bill Walker ran on the Alaska First Unity ticket with Democrat Byron Mallott as his lieutenant governor choice (lieutenant governors are like a vice president but for the state-level government). The state's Democratic Party did not run their own official candidate for governor, leaving Walker to primarily contend with then-lieutenant governor Republican Sean Parnell.

Walker won the election with 134,658 votes to Parnell's 128,435, with about 16,000 votes going to either the Libertarian or Constitution tickets. This installed Walker as the country's only independent governor from 2015 to 2019. Yet the tenure came crashing to an end as Walker lost his re-election bid in a three-way race, suspending his campaign not even a month before the election. Any chance he had had already faded away.[88] [89] [90]

While it did not result in an independent victory, the 2010 Maine election for governor is another prominent example of a respectable independent performance, and in a three-way race no less. Maine, like Alaska, is another politically quirky state with more robust independent politics than typically found in the rest of the country. Eliot R. Cutler made a strong bid in the race by garnering 35.9 percent of the vote, blasting past Democrat Elizabeth Mitchell's 18.8 percent and coming close to Republican Paul LePage's 37.6 percent.

Two other independent candidates combined for another 6 percent of the vote, possibly indicating that Cutler could very well have defeated Paul LePage and become an independent governor (though it is not certain, as we do not know *why* exactly those independents were voted for).[91] LePage won a second term in 2014.

There are far too many local governments to cover in a single book, but independents can make some noise at that level as well, depending on the locality. It could be for mayor, county commissions, school boards, city councils, or special governmental districts like a water management district. Keep in mind, however, that many of these elections are *nominally* nonpartisan, even though the candidates are usually backed by Republican or Democratic organizations. When someone is called an independent here, we mean someone who is either a third-party or nonparty candidate in an office that is officially partisan. Therefore, this does not count officially *nonpartisan* offices. As of June 1, 2021, four of the top one hundred cities in population were led by independent mayors.[92]

Independent Candidates as a Whole

Citizens advocating for more officeholders that are independent of the two main parties might be eager to point to these successes as evidence of how independents are competitive, but the reality is that the vast majority have no chance at winning elections. While most of this book covers institutional and voter-related roadblocks, the issues do not stop there. Many independent candidates are not just uncompetitive; they are downright awful candidates.

This inevitably becomes a more subjective discussion,

especially when commentators use the vague term "electability." Many partisans and ideologues, or even those less attached to a party and/or ideology, may belittle a candidate because of what their stances are on issues, but there are more objective ways to evaluate a candidate's viability. These qualities are arguably even more important for independent candidates. Here are some considerations:

- What is on their resumé?
- How much do they know and understand about politics?
- Are they able to formulate an effective, or at least sound, campaign strategy?
- How good are they at communicating their message?
- Can they break through the noise and convince voters they are a "real" option?
- Do they come across as a serious candidate or just goofy?

The truth is that there are many independent candidates that utterly fail at most or all these criteria and more. It is not entirely on them, of course. It could be more a matter of ballot access, the media rarely deciding to cover them, the sparse set of independent political operatives available compared to Republican or Democratic ones, or something else. It could be any combination of these things.

Yet some of the bigger names stumble the few times they do get the spotlight. Howard Schultz, the former CEO of Starbucks, teased a run for president in the 2020 election. While he never made an official declaration for candidacy, he made several major mistakes and was sharply criticized for some of his comments. Criticisms included rebukes of policy ideas, comments about race, claiming he had spent more time with the military than any other presidential candidates despite then-contenders Tulsi Gabbard and Pete Buttigieg (who served in the armed forces themselves), and he was reluctant to say he would divest his shares in Starbucks.[93] Fair or not, these moments reinforced many voters' perceptions of a third choice as an unaffordable choice to make. When you have as little room for error as an independent candidate does, everything you do is magnified even more so.

Even those independent candidates who are credible often approach the campaigns the wrong way. Almost every time, they try too hard to appeal to the fact that many people are sick of the two main political parties. Clearly, it rarely ever works because most voters still tend to choose the Republican or Democrat. That suggests that most independents do not understand much about the psychology of voters.

"Real" versus "Fake" Independents

Besides the varying reasons people have for identifying themselves as independents, there is another potential problem: "fake" independents, for lack of a better term. Many candidates of a third party or no party genuinely see themselves that way, but there are some candidates that run as independents when they would never characterize themselves as one. If that is the case, why would they not just run with the Democrats or Republicans in the election?

There are a couple of tactical reasons why these would-be Republican or Democratic candidates would run as independents. For one, their analysis of the race says to them that they have no chance of securing a party nomination against some other formidable contender. Thus, they give themselves a shot straight to the general election by filing to run as a nonparty candidate. For two, they may have run in the party's primary and lost, but the filing deadlines for candidacy still allow them to file for the race again as an independent. To prevent this, many states have passed what are known as "sore loser" laws, which prevent a primary election loser from trying to run as a third option in the general election. In these cases, once that candidate has lost in the primary, they are completely done for that election.

Independent Campaign Organizations and Operatives

Sometimes, organizations advocating or directly campaigning for independent candidates take the wrong approach as well. Among the biggest mistakes they make is the misinterpretation of polling results, namely (1) voters' openness to independents candidates and (2) the proportion of people wanting a legitimate third party to contend. On the surface, these statistics, such as those from Pew and Gallup research, may look like they bode well, but if they were that important, we would be seeing many more independent officeholders than we do now.

Many independent campaign operatives and advocates do not have enough understanding of voter psychology to have success. Even if they did, that would not necessarily guarantee more victories since there are so many other cards in the electoral process that are stacked against independents. Yet it would give them better chances to take an in-depth dive into the studies and practical lessons regarding psychology. Some key challenges include the following.

- The candidate must truly break through the "wasted vote" mentality.

- They must solve the knowledge gap problem, as independents are usually little known and drowned out by the big kids in the two major parties.

- They need to understand how risk-taking analyses work, convincing potential voters that it would be a risk to *not* vote for the independent.

- They need to recognize that the description of "independent" is too vague, and you cannot treat all independents the same because they can have wildly different political views and definitions of their independence.

This is not meant to be a knock on any of these operatives or groups. Some are great at what they do with what is at their disposal. Some of them do know about the psychological elements regarding how voters view independents. Some of them are fully cognizant of all the natural weaknesses of independent campaigns regarding money, access to expertise, infrastructure, etc. Knowing these things does not mean a much greater chance of victory. Yet there are also many of these independent candidates and organizations who do not understand just how many factors are at play and how they affect the chances of independent election victories.

One of the biggest stumbling blocks for independent advocates, candidates, organizations, and political operatives is this overreliance and hyper-focus on public opinion polls showing a large proportion of voters being open to independents. It seems to be a driving force for those working to get independents elected; they use it to signify the strength of independents. This may not seem like a problem at first.

After all, they must first be willing to vote for an independent before officially picking them, right?

There is a big problem with that conclusion: *thinking* about doing something is vastly different from actually doing that thing. Polls show widespread consideration of an independent candidate in elections all the time, but rarely does it come to fruition as a vote cast. Many people know they are upset with both the Republican and Democratic Parties, but do they know if they would actually vote for someone else? The answer is mostly no. The questions are not typically framed in a way that gauges the voters' likelihood of selecting an independent candidate or why they are thinking about an independent.

There is also the potential issue of how the poll itself asks the question about openness to third options. The wording and phrasing of poll questions are so critical to its validity that changing merely one word can garner completely different results. If the poll question asks if someone is "open" to an independent candidate, that doesn't inherently mean anything about physically voting for them. Asking about the "likelihood" of voting for an independent might get a more usable answer to work with, but it still does not quite translate into actual votes.

The problem could also lie with the respondents themselves. It might be a social desirability bias at play, so they claim they are an independent or would consider voting for one to avoid judgment from peers. That does not mean that only a small proportion of people are truly contemplating an independent, though. That depends on many other factors like what elected office is being campaigned for and where it is. The point is that not everyone has the same reason(s) for responding that they are open to voting for independent candidates, just as they do not have the same reason(s) for self-identifying as independents. It is a potential pitfall to watch out for.

Summary

Obviously, there must be an independent candidate running in an election for voters to potentially choose them. While many voters may say they would consider an independent, it does not mean they will just choose any of them that run. Independent candidates themselves falter due to mistakes they make in the campaign, forces outside of their control, or both. Sometimes operatives and campaign organizations for independent candidates stumble as well. In a political environment that is so geared toward two-party dominance, every action those independent candidates take is that much more critical to having a chance at winning.

While the elements in this chapter are all important regardless of which election it is, the impact they have is not the same across the board. The effectiveness of independent candidates and campaign organizations generally varies based on the type of election in question—which is the topic of the next chapter.

Chapter 6

Independent Election Results by Type of Election

Independents have a problem with just about every type of election—some elections more than others.

Every year, thousands of elections are held across the United States at all levels of government. Countless voters flood the polls to make their voices heard. While presidential election years—and to a lesser extent, midterm election years—get all the publicity, odd-numbered years also hold elections, especially local ones. Louisiana, Mississippi, New Jersey, and Virginia even have their state legislative elections in odd-numbered years. Sometimes, regularly scheduled elections do not even happen in November, but in another month like May.

The divisions of party affiliations in the US House have a somewhat strange history. (For simplicity and relevancy's sake, we will just focus on the years where it has been Democrats versus Republicans). From the thirty-fifth Congress (1857 to 1859) until roughly around the end of

World War II, the number of representatives from third parties that won election fluctuated considerably multiple times (e.g., around twenty representatives to less than a handful).[94]

Post-World War II, there have never been more than two independents that won a US House election, and no third parties have won an election since 1965. From 1965 to 1991, and 2007 to the present, no independents have won at all.[95] (Former Representative Justin Amash became a Libertarian toward the end of his last term, but he won elections as a Republican. He did not run in 2020 at all.)

State legislatures, on the other hand, have sometimes had much more colorful and wild histories of third-party and nonparty election winners, though this mostly comes from state houses. The Vermont State House's history, for example, is littered with nonparty and various third-party election winners.[96] While they are still severely outnumbered by the two major parties, you can still find some third-party and nonparty state legislators today. In the 2020 state legislative elections, two third-party senators won in Vermont and twenty-six third-party or nonparty representatives won in eight different states.[97]

All of this is to demonstrate that while third-party and nonparty candidates still have little success at winning elections, there are different rates of success for them depending on where you go in the country. The basic parameters of these elections can have a significant impact on whether an independent wins or loses.

How Do We Delineate Types of Elections?

Circumstances unique to each election aside, we can make some general comparisons based on the same or a similar category even if they are not completely one-to-one. One way we break them down is by federal, state, and local elections. By "federal," we mean Congress and the presidential/vice presidential ticket. By "state," we mean state executives (e.g., governor, attorney general, treasurer, etc.), which are statewide offices, and state legislators. By "local," we mean various offices like county commissioners, city councils, school boards, special districts (e.g., water), and others that are narrow and closest to the community level. While independents have trouble winning elections in general, they do have varying degrees of success based on what level of election is in question.

Other electoral system-specific factors also play a key role concerning the success of independents. While elections that are inherently partisan get almost all the attention, there are many nonpartisan elections where the candidates are not allowed to officially run as a member of a party. Various types of primary systems—the primary elections that occur before general elections—also generally have different effects on independent candidates and voters because they vary in how they function and how voters participate. Other elements include whether it is a special election or a regularly scheduled election, whether the seat is open or held by an incumbent, and whether the winner is based on plurality or majority voting.

Federal versus State versus Local Elections

It may be surprising to some readers how many third-party and nonpartisan officeholders there are in state legislatures, even though close to all the seats are still held by Republicans and Democrats. Vermont, for example, has an ample number of members of the Vermont Progressive Party in its legislature, though they still tend to align with the Democrats, given that they are on the same side of the ideological spectrum.

Generally speaking, the lower you go in government levels, the more often you will find independent officeholders. There are a lot more opportunities and many different realities (e.g., how many voters align with each political party, if any, economic differences, elected officials representing a district) depending on the district. There are bound to be a few state legislative districts more inclined to vote for a third-party or nonparty candidate, as has been demonstrated. There are thousands and thousands of local-level offices, so you will find some independents somewhere.

Partisan versus (Ostensibly) Nonpartisan Races

Some elections are nominally nonpartisan, where no one officially runs as a member of *any* party, even if they are normally affiliated with one. Nobody appears as a candidate of a party on the ballot—only their name appears. Most nonpartisan elections are for local offices, such as many school boards, though not all are. Nebraska is the only state with a nonpartisan state legislature. (It is also the only unicameral one, with just a senate and no house.) Some higher state-level offices, like some state supreme courts, also have candidates run on the ballot with no official party affiliation.

Yet sometimes, the "nonpartisan" label is only nominal. Many of these elections still have the Republican and Democratic Parties getting involved. Candidates may officially be registered *as a voter* with one of the parties, they may be known to normally affiliate with that party, and the parties will spend money on the races and endorse candidates. This is not always the case, but if the race is considered important enough, it is likely the parties will get involved. In truth, while Nebraska's state legislators all run in officially nonpartisan elections, their would-be partisan affiliations can be gauged by their voter registration, member lists from the state Republican and Democratic Parties, and endorsements from the state and local parties.[98]

Theoretically, "true" independent candidates would have an easier time in these elections, but that is not necessarily true. They will still often lose out to candidates backed by major party money who have greater means to reach out to voters. It also tends to be the most hard-core of voters—who tend to be more partisan and ideological than average—that pay attention to and participate in the most local elections. These voters will still often see the partisan and ideological cues, like local party backing of candidates, to guide their decision-making.[99] Thus, nonpartisan races are often still a steep hill to climb for independents.

Types of Primary Systems

For simplification purposes, much of this book is concerned with independents running in general elections and against both a Republican and a Democrat unless noted otherwise. That said, it is important to note exceptions to this rule as primaries can have a monumental impact on independent chances of victory.

Most general elections will have primaries sometime beforehand, and there are various types depending on the state, the level of the election (e.g., Congress, state legislative), and political party bylaws. Each one has wildly varying impacts on how much independent voters can influence an election. It is also possible for the Republican Party to use one kind of primary in one type of race in one state while the Democratic Party uses a different kind of primary in the same race in the same state. Each state might also handle the same kind of primary different from another state.

- **Closed primary:** This is the only type of primary where independent voters have absolutely no say because they cannot vote, unless a "recognized" third party in a state runs a primary and has multiple candidates vying for its nomination. Only party members can vote in closed primaries and for their registered party only, meaning independents not registered with a recognized political party must wait until the general election to cast a ballot (unless the other major party lets independents vote in their primary).

- **Semi-closed primary:** A more relaxed version of the closed primary, nonparty voters can participate with the party's registered voters in an election. However, voters registered with a party must still vote in that party's primary and cannot cross over to a different party's primary. In fifteen states, at least one party uses a semi-closed primary for congressional and/or state-level elections.[100]

- **Open primary:** Anybody can vote in open primaries.

A voter privately declares which party's ballot they are casting for at the polls and then receives said ballot. There are twenty-one states where at least one party uses this method for congressional- and/or state-level elections.[101]

- **Semi-open primary:** This is effectively the same as an open primary, but in a semi-open format each voter must make a public declaration of which party's primary they are choosing.[102] Public does not mean yelling to the world, "Look at me, I'm voting in this primary!" Rather, a voter will have to officially change their affiliation at the polls on Election Day before they can vote in that party's primary.

- **Top-two primary:** The top-two vote-getters move to the general election, regardless of how many votes either of them received. Washington, California, and Nebraska use this type of system for congressional and/or state-level elections. (Nebraska only uses it for its state legislature.) Alaska stands out in yet another instance here—voters in 2020 approved a ballot measure that included a provision for top-*four* partisan primaries.[103]

- **"Jungle"/blanket primary:** Although it is mostly a matter of semantics and is therefore arguable which is which, top-two primaries and blanket primaries are sometimes referred to as "jungle" primaries. Blanket primaries are almost the exact same system as top-two primaries. The difference is that in regular top-two primaries, there will always be two competitors that go to the general election regardless of how many primary votes they received. However, in what *this book* considers a "true" jungle primary, a candidate can win the election outright if they capture a majority of the primary votes. Thus, the blanket primary can technically be considered a general election, and the actual general election could be considered a run-off. Louisiana is the only state that uses this system.

How These Primary Systems Can Affect Independents

It is difficult to come up with reliable statistics on how exactly these primary systems boost or hinder independent candidates' chances of victory, especially in relation to each other. Sometimes, it is a matter of a small sample size: there are not enough instances of a given type of primary to compare to other types. There are also so many other factors intertwined that would confound the data and make it challenging to pick apart: how many independent and total candidates are running, what level of office the election is, lack of data on voter registration statistics, how much independent campaigns differ from each other, and more. Nevertheless, many political scientists have still attempted to do this very thing.

We can, however, approach this from a more theoretical angle—how an independent campaign should evaluate it. What primary systems could we generally expect to be more helpful to independent campaigns? What other dynamics within a given primary system could significantly impact those chances?

The most straightforward aspect to look at is which of these primary systems can independent candidates even participate in. The only ways that *nonparty* affiliated candidates can run in a primary are if it is a top-two or blanket format—otherwise, they just go to the general election. If a third party has multiple candidates running and is an "official" party in the state in question, they can hold the other types of primaries—though most times, they only have one candidate of their own running anyway. Thus, for the most part, third parties will be locked out of any primary outside of the top-two and blanket formats. Independent *voters* can at least participate in open primaries, and in certain cases, semi-closed primaries.

Independents' chances in top-two and blanket primaries, however, can greatly differ depending on the seat. For example, how does the total number of Republicans, Democrats, and other *voters* in a district stack up? That is going to affect the proportion of voters who are naturally going to be more open to voting for an independent candidate.

Then you must consider how many Republican, Democratic, and other *candidates* run in an election. If there are only one or two independents but a bunch of Republicans and Democrats running, those partisan candidates may split enough votes between them that an independent candidate takes one of the top two spots. For example, let us say that there are a total of 60,000 votes for Democrats and 30,000 for Republicans in a single race.

- If there were only two Democrats and two Republicans, there is still a substantial chance that Democrats take both top-two spots to guarantee a Democratic winner in the general election. Each Democrat might get around 30,000 votes, and each Republican might get around 15,000 votes, or something close to this.

- Now, if that same race had *six* Democrats against two Republicans, there is a reasonable likelihood that those Democrats will split the votes enough to the point that one or both Republicans get the top-two spots. Each Republican might still get around 15,000 votes, but each Democrat might only get 10,000 votes, or something close to this.

When there is a fear of this kind of scenario happening, state and relevant local Republican and Democratic Parties may get involved, trying to persuade a candidate or two on their side of the aisle to drop out, so the party has a better chance of winning. Sometimes, the candidates who are asked to drop out will oblige but not always. In any case, this might represent a prime opportunity for an independent candidate. (Of course, that also partly depends on *how many* independent candidates run as well. With how varied independents can be in where their politics lie and what label they run under, it is not necessarily likely that they will cooperate to see who among them is willing to drop out of the race).

Open versus Incumbent-Held Seats

To the best of my knowledge, there are, unfortunately, no in-depth examinations of how different the success rates of independent candidates are based on whether they defeated an incumbent or were vying for an open seat. Either way, the number of examples of either scenario would probably be too few and/or spread out over time to be able to make an empirical claim one way or the other. Nevertheless, there is reasonable speculation to be made as long as we keep in mind that it is just that—speculation.

The incumbency advantage for Republicans and

Democrats is well-documented, however. Already being an occupant of an elected seat is a big boost to one's chances of winning by virtue of name recognition and resources that come with holding the office already.[104] [105] [106] Since independent candidates tend to be at a significant disadvantage in those regards already, it will be a particularly hard hill to climb for them. Their hopes for election victory would generally be more warranted in open seats because it is likely to be a more even playing field for independents to contend in. Of course, some Republican and Democratic contenders will still have far more financial resources, connections, name recognition, and possibly experience in campaigns, but at least independent candidates would not have to worry about the incumbency advantage in those cases.

Ranked-Choice Voting

Ranked-choice voting (RCV) has slowly been gaining steam in some parts of the country, most notably in Maine. In ranked-choice voting, voters rank all the candidates in order of who they most want to win. If no candidate wins a majority of the votes, the candidate receiving the lowest number of votes is eliminated, and the second-place votes are counted. If that still does not lead to a win by majority vote, the next candidate with the least number of votes is eliminated, and the third-place votes are counted. This process continues until one of the candidates claims a majority of the votes. A voter is not necessarily required to rank every candidate in the race.

(RCV is also sometimes called "instant run-off" voting. Normally, in elections that require a majority-vote winner, the top two candidates move on to a run-off election that occurs soon after the normal election. This can happen in both primaries and general elections. In RCV, however, there is just one election, and the next round of choices is counted right then and there, instead of voters having to come back to the polls another day to vote. Hence, the run-off is "instant.")

Ranked-choice voting is a relatively new phenomenon. As of March 2021, except for Maine's implementation of RCV for federal- and state-level elections and Alaska's adoption but not yet implementation for federal- and state-level general elections, almost every instance of RCV in the country was for municipal elections.[107] Since there are too few occurrences of RCV—and they are too far spread out across the country, so each city could have other wildly varying impacts from each other—it is difficult, if not impossible, to have a reliable empirical conclusion as to whether RCV helps or hinders independents.

From a theoretical point of view, RCV could represent prime opportunities for independents to claim election victories. Independents are *usually* not going to be adamantly opposed by voters, but rather they will be a second, third, etc., priority. Voters also do not need to rank every candidate, and with how partisan many voters are, they probably will not even rank the opposing party's candidate. If the independent garners enough votes in the first round of voting to prevent a majority winner while also staving off their own elimination, they could potentially have enough second-round or even third-round votes (if a third round is needed) to pull off the win.

Here is a simple example to illustrate the above. In a real election, it will not look this clean.

	Repub-lican	Democrat	Inde-pendent	Other candidate
1st round total	**1,000**	**1,000**	**800**	**200**
2nd round votes	600	500	1,000	Eliminated
2nd round total	**1,600**	**1,500**	**1,800**	**Eliminated**
3rd round votes	700	Eliminated	900	Eliminated
3rd round total	**2,300**	**Eliminated**	**2,700**	**Eliminated**
WINNER: Independent Candidate				

This by no means guarantees, or even promises, that independents will win. Obviously, this will depend greatly on other factors like how many party-affiliated and nonparty-affiliated voters there are, the candidates themselves, and how voters perceive the independent. There will likely need to be at least another independent candidate, whether that is another nonparty affiliate or a third-party, to be knocked out of the running, as the main independent is unlikely to get enough first-round votes to overtake the Republican or Democrat. From this theoretical view, however, it shows how the system could perhaps benefit those (likely centrist) independent candidates in their quest for public office.

Plurality-Vote versus Majority-Vote Elections

Many single-member district elections just need a plurality—where a candidate simply needs the most votes to win a seat (multi-member districts, by default, only need a plurality because there are two or more seats up for election in the district). Other elections, however, require candidates to take more than 50 percent of the votes to win. If no candidate captures a majority of votes in these elections, the top two (or however many as designated by law) vote-getters move to a run-off election held weeks after. This can happen for both primary and general elections.

To the best of my knowledge, there are no substantive studies looking at long-term trends of whether plurality or majority-vote systems are more beneficial for independent candidates. That is probably partially due to majority-vote systems being much less common in the US. It is also somewhat difficult to approach this theoretically. In plurality systems, enough candidates participating and splitting the vote amongst themselves *might* be enough for an independent candidate to win, but since they win so rarely anyway, it is hard to say when and where this is the case.

With majority systems, there often are not enough people for independent candidates to draw from (at least, reliably). The voters more likely to vote for independent candidates—moderate members of other parties and "true" independents—also vote less often.[108] [109] It might work out better for independent candidates if they have only one opponent, either a Republican or Democrat, but that is a majority-vote election by default since it is just two candidates running.

Summary

Beyond the psychology of voters and the actions of independent candidates and organizations, the structure of elections plays a key role in the successes and failures of independents running for public office. While those elements obviously affect how the different types of elections play out, the election types themselves also exert a major amount of influence on their own regarding the success rates of independent candidates. The lower the level of election it is in question, the more likely it is that there are independent candidates that have won public office. The effect of other elements, such as the type of primary and whether it is a partisan or nominally nonpartisan race, is murkier.

The type of election also plays a major role in how campaigns are and should be conducted—which leads us to our next topic on how independent candidates' campaign operations compare to those of Republicans and Democrats. Some of the basics are similar for each, but as you will find out, independent candidates are hamstrung while trying to keep up with their partisan counterparts.

Chapter 7

Unique Roadblocks to Independent Campaigns

Independents have a problem with the fundamentals of political campaigns.

Every campaign for office should have a written-out or typed campaign plan. In a way, these plans tell a story about the district (or state, if it is a statewide race like for governor). Without going too deeply into the minor details, these plans cover every aspect of the race you must account for while allowing for some flexibility in the event of unforeseen circumstances on the campaign trail. These elements include the following:[110]

- Each candidate's strengths and weaknesses (even your own candidate because you need to prepare for the opposition's attacks),

- Strategy and tactics in targeting voters (which ones, how often, when, and with what methods, such as TV or radio),

- The demographic and partisan makeup of the district (if the data is available), and
- Cost projections for the campaign

For one of my classes in my first semester of graduate school, the final project was to make a full-blown campaign plan. My classmates and I were all given the same race, one which was likely going to be competitive, and we were assigned either the Republican or Democrat as if we were working for them (though each of us worked on our own plan). We had to scour through things like the aforementioned elements, the history of the district's elections, and more. While there were no specific requirements for the number of pages or words needed, we had to make sure we included all the elements of the campaign we needed. The final document was beefy, but if we were campaign professionals doing this for a living with more resources, the plan would have been even more in-depth.

That project was an especially relevant one to my internship. Though I did not make a full campaign plan there, I had to research and analyze many of the elements included in one. Since then, I have thought about campaign plans regarding how independent candidates and operatives should approach them. I found that, in most races, independents are either greatly disadvantaged at (or fail to properly account for) almost all these aspects.

Many candidates simply jump into a race without truly understanding how the process of a campaign works, and it is not just independents. There are many Republicans and Democrats who do that too. If you do not account for what Republicans and Democrats tend to have at their disposal that independents do not, it will not be a fun time as an independent candidate, campaign professional, or advocate.

Targeting Voters

Different demographics of voters generally respond in different ways to campaigns; some will be much more likely to vote Democrat, and others are much more likely to vote Republican. These can shift somewhat depending on the election. For example, there might be a higher than usual percentage of Cuban voters, who are usually more likely to vote Republican, that might vote Democratic in a particular district's election. In many cases, campaigns will either have an internal database that tracks voters that are likely to support them, or they can contact counties' Supervisor of Elections offices to get a registered voter list. If it is a state that keeps track of what party a voter is registered with (some states simply register voters, and that's it), then the list will show what their party affiliation is.

However, there are a lot of campaigners that do not understand how the campaign should be run. They do not realize that there is a serious "method to the madness" in how campaigns work. You do not just send campaign material to voters randomly and hope for the best—not if you want to be successful, at least. You need some intuition about how the voters you are trying to reach think and feel.

A physical, written/typed campaign plan is of critical importance. This wide-ranging document is supposed to address just about everything that will affect the campaign (though it has some flexibility so that you can account for unforeseen developments on the way to Election Day). Here are just a few examples of what is included in campaign plans.[111] [112]

- **What medium(s) of communication do you use to reach out to voters, and which voters do you target with each?** Mediums include television, radio, campaign mailers, and social media. Each of these has strengths and weaknesses based on who they reach, how much they cost, how much you can hone it to target specific groups, etc. Groups of people respond differently to each medium.

- **How often do you contact people?** Just about every single one of us may hate the incessant campaign ads that we are inundated with, but the truth is repetition works. A professor of mine from graduate school puts it this way: Why do Coke and Pepsi constantly have commercials when so many people already know about their existence? They already have name recognition. The reason is they want to constantly be on your mind in hopes that you think, "You know what? I could *really* go for a soda right now," and then you go buy some. Political campaigns are similar in this regard. You might know who they are, but they are trying to frequently be at the forefront of your mind to make sure you cast a vote for them. They're trying to ensure brand loyalty.

- **When do you contact voters?** You have probably noticed that the campaign ads tend to exponentially increase the closer to an election we are. Which voters you contact at what point is another key to winning a campaign, especially in a media environment where endless stimuli are trying to grab our attention. Outreach that is too early may not be that effective, but it depends on the voters.

What does all this have to do with independent candidates and campaign organizations? First, they generally seem to have less understanding of these finer details, over-relying on the fact that a significant proportion of voters are frustrated with the two main parties and believing that will inherently tip the scales in favor of independents.

Second, independents usually have less access to seasoned political operatives and robust research resources that significantly benefit a campaign. For example, the two main parties have extremely in-depth databases of their own for tracking potential voters. Independents, meanwhile, are more often relegated to the broad voter lists that county Supervisors of Elections and state departments of elections provide or have a much less-developed database of their own. The rules for requesting voter lists vary greatly by state, such as who is allowed to access the voter lists, the kinds of information they contain about voters, and how exactly they should be requested and received.[113] Therefore, this can be an even bigger disadvantage for independent candidates depending on which state is in question.

Third, it is naturally much harder for candidates not associated with either Democrats or Republicans to craft a strategy, and the two main parties have a lot of regular tropes they employ that you often see in messaging. For example, you often see, "the opposing party's candidate is a radical." As we talked about in Chapter 4, independent candidates have far fewer heuristics at their disposal, and they are significantly less effective ones.

Fourth, it is usually much easier to figure out who is a Republican and who is a Democrat through clues that are not necessarily political in nature. For example, the kinds of magazines that they read and some non-ideological or nonpartisan political bumper stickers can be surprisingly indicative of a voter's political leanings. But it is much harder to gauge who is an independent voter in this manner. There are few of these clues that you can point to as evidence of an independent leaning, let alone what *kind* of independent they are.

Voter Turnout

Compared to other countries with free elections, US election turnout is relatively quite low.[114] The voters who make it to the polls tend to have certain qualities—be it demographics, attitudes, or something else—that distinguish them from nonvoters.

The Republican and Democratic Parties may not sit well with many voters, but their members vote at much higher rates than independents. Even if they are dissatisfied with their party, partisan affiliation is the number one indicator of a voter's choice in an election. Furthermore, the "strong" Republicans or Democrats are more likely to vote than their "weak" counterparts. "Strong" in this sense means someone who more closely identifies with their party label. Independents, and people that would likely be more inclined to vote for an independent, show up to the polls at much lower rates than stronger partisan voters do.[115] [116] This leads to a predictable outcome for independent candidates.

So, why do independents and weaker partisans tend to vote less often? The strong partisans generally have a lot more investment in election outcomes. If you are heavily involved in politics—volunteering for door-to-door campaigns, phone banking, going to your county's political party meetings regularly, attending town halls, etc.—it is clearly important for you to do whatever you can to help carry your "team" and preferred candidates to victory, so you would not miss casting your ballot. Stronger partisans often see elections as an existential crisis between good and evil—if the "other side" wins, the country is "done for." Meanwhile, weak partisans and independents generally do not have as much investment in election outcomes.[117] [118] It is not that they do not care, obviously, but they *usually* do not perceive there to be as much at stake as strong partisans would and/or are more apathetic.

That poses an enormous problem for independent candidates. A sizable proportion of their would-be voters do not even turn out. If they do, many of them are resigned to voting for the "lesser evil" from either the Republican or Democratic Parties due to the psychological aspects discussed in Chapter 4. Some independents really are not predisposed to voting for independent candidates. Hence, despite the proportion of Americans who identify as independent and are registered with a third party or no party, you constantly see non-major party candidates make barely a dent in election results.

Persuasion versus Mobilization

One of the most basic, overarching concerns of campaigns is this: is it about persuasion or mobilization? By persuasion, we mean convincing voters to choose one side, when there is a good chance they would not have done so had the candidate's campaign not reached out to them. As divisive as politics can be and as completely set in their ways as some voters are, there are still voters out there that can and need to be appealed to.

By mobilization, we mean galvanizing the voter base a campaign already has so they come out to vote. Just because a voter would choose the candidate does not mean they will physically cast a ballot. Hard-core Republicans and Democrats do not need to be pushed to vote—they are already going to no matter what—but those that are less politically active may need the impetus.

Note that persuasion and mobilization are not mutually exclusive. They rarely are, if ever. Still, a campaign is usually going to need an emphasis on one or the other. Every race has a unique set of circumstances, so the answer will not be the same for each one.

Where do independents come into play here? They are usually going to have to focus on persuasion, specifically of Republican and Democratic voters. Independent voters, be they third-party or no party, are an eclectic group and aren't all looking for the same kind of independent candidate, and they do not turn out to vote at the same rates that Republicans and Democrats do. So, even if independent voters were a more unified front, those that do turn out will almost always be outnumbered by Republicans and Democrats that show up to vote. Mobilizing independent voters won't be enough, though it is still necessary. The composition of Republican and Democratic voter bases are also much more obvious than that of an independent. Therefore, independent candidates have to persuade enough Republican and Democratic voters that they are not only the kind of candidate those voters are looking for but that voting for them is not a waste.

Infrastructure of Major Parties versus Independents

The Republican and Democratic Parties have an enormous number of moving gears in their operations, staggered at the federal, state, and local levels of government. There are, of course, the national Republican and Democratic Parties with campaign-oriented arms, such as the National Republican Senatorial Committee (NRSC) and the Democratic Congressional Campaign Committee (DCCC). Below them are the state parties. Even in states where they are generally uncompetitive (such as the Democratic Party in Wyoming or the Republican Party in Oregon), there will be affiliated state branches that focus on races for state government. Every single county in the United States also has a Republican and Democratic Party that operates at that level, and many cities will also have their own version of the party.

Each of these levels works with each other to some extent. The national parties tend to be more involved at the federal level, the state parties at the state level, and the local parties at the local level. Depending on the race, however, they may work in tandem. National and state level parties may work together to get US Senate candidates elected, as US Senate candidates represent an entire state and are voted on only by the state they would represent. The state parties may work with local parties on key elections like an important state legislative race or the mayor of a major city.

Outside of the "official" party structures are grassroots groups and individuals that are clearly affiliated with the Republican and Democratic Parties and may even directly work together with the parties but are technically not part of the official campaign machine.

- One of the most visible of these groups is College

Republicans and College Democrats. They are established in most higher education institutions. If you have taken classes at the college/university level, you have likely heard of these groups.

- Some of the wealthiest big-name individual donors are almost, if not always, donating to one party or the other. Sheldon Adelson, the former CEO of the Las Vegas Sands Corporation, was one of the biggest contributors to Republican Party campaign operations. Tom Steyer, who ran a brief presidential campaign in 2020, is one of the biggest donors on the Democratic side.

- Some interest groups, activist groups, and political action committees (PACs) heavily lean toward one party and will essentially campaign for candidates in that party, sometimes even recruiting them.

The infrastructure for independent candidates pales in comparison. Third parties will sometimes have a state-level affiliate, and only the most widespread ones like the Libertarian Party will have a national version. They will also have some county-level parties in states where that third party exists. But these operations are not even remotely as robust as those for the Democratic and Republican Parties. There are far fewer activist groups and PACs devoted to candidates of these parties. They will not appear all over the states that they exist in. Colleges will not have nearly as many student groups that are in direct support of a third party, though you may sometimes see a College Libertarians group, for example.

For candidates who are running as no party at all, things get even trickier. By nature, it is not a straightforward answer as to who naturally backs their campaign operations, though that is not to say that there are not any at all. Arguably, the most prominent organization for nonparty affiliates is Unite America. Unite America counts Republicans, Democrats, and independents among its ranks, contributing not only to various independent campaign operations but to nonpartisan initiatives such as independent redistricting reforms, more adoptions of ranked-choice voting, and nonpartisan primaries.[119]

Beyond Unite America, there are few, if any, major nonpartisan organizations that are heavily involved in independent political candidates' campaigns. They do have some partners such as FairVote, Bridge Alliance, and the Leadership Now project.[120] But these groups are not necessarily involved in the actual campaigning for independent candidates. The Republican and Democratic Party apparatuses are also exponentially larger than that of Unite America—they are practically everywhere, while Unite America is not even close to that. It is always harder to compete when you are a far smaller, completely overshadowed group with limited reach.

Creating a "Bench" of Talent

There is much about politics that is well-suited toward sports analogies. In professional sports, there are the top leagues that everyone pays attention to (NFL, NBA, MLB, NHL, etc.). Each one has some form of a "farm system" used to develop players who have potential but are not quite ready for the top level of the sport. Major League Baseball has the minor leagues of A, AA, and AAA baseball, the National Hockey League has a couple of lower-level leagues, and so on. Eventually, a small proportion of those prospects will be called up to the big leagues.

The Republican and Democratic Parties, in a sense, have their own sort of "farm system." City or county affiliates might recruit community or business leaders to run for, say, the city council or the state house. The state affiliates may groom incumbent state legislators or community and business leaders well-known throughout the state in question. The national-level parties might directly help statewide officials (e.g., governor or state attorney general) prepare them for a run for Congress or possibly even the US presidency. Such groups include the National Republican Senate Committee (NRSC) and the Democratic Congressional Campaign Committee (DCCC, usually said as "D Triple-C").

The major parties have built their infrastructures over the course of many years, enabling them to create systems in which they can train candidates they recruit. The infrastructures of independent political operations are paltry in comparison—not to mention fragmented across many third parties and completely nonpartisan candidates. Third parties have a small semblance of a "farm system" at best. They are not influential enough, do not have enough members, and/or do not have the money to effectively train and mentor would-be political candidates anywhere near what the Republican and Democratic Parties do.

Beyond Unite America, there really is not much else for independents when it comes to cultivating prospects for office. It takes a considerable number of resources and coordination to develop talent. This limits just how much nonparty and third-party organizations can do for that purpose and continually reinforces the divide between them and the major parties, since the latter is far more capable of grooming future candidates for office or current officeholders for even higher office.

Summary

Independent campaigns share some basic similarities with Republican and Democratic ones in terms of what they need to know and do to reach voters. Yet independents are often much less aware of what some of those basics are and how they must adjust their approach. Disadvantages in how they can target and turn out voters, the infrastructure and coordination of their political apparatuses, and the ability to mentor candidates for office in the future are just some of the reasons why.

There are also some more unique issues that face independent candidates that are ingrained in the political system, governed more so by particular rules and laws. Such impediments are the focus of the next chapter.

Chapter 8

Unique Roadblocks to Independent Candidates and Parties

Independents have a problem with electoral roadblocks baked into their campaigns that are more unique to them but not necessarily inherent to the system.

During my graduate school internship, a couple of projects we worked on involved getting two nonparty candidates, both from a different state, onto their respective ballots for the 2018 election. One of these would-be candidates was in Indiana, and the other was in Texas. This part of the election process is referred to as ballot access (certain rules to follow and certain thresholds to meet to get on the ballot, typically a filing fee and/or a minimum number of petition nomination signatures).[121] [122]

For this project, I had to do some research as to just how many signatures were needed, as the filing fee option was not available to nonparty candidates. For the Texas candidate running for the US Senate, the difference in the number of signatures required for his independent candidacy compared to Republicans and Democrats was staggering. For the 2018 election, a major party candidate for the US Senate could pay either a $5,000 filing fee or gather 5,000 valid petition signatures.[123] Meanwhile, nonparty candidates' only option was to gather a number of signatures equal to at least one percent of all votes cast in the previous Texas gubernatorial election, which was held in 2014.[124] There were just over 4.7 million votes cast in that race, meaning the campaign needed to gather more than 47,000 petition signatures to get the candidate on the ballot.[125]

It was a similar situation for the candidate in Indiana—who, if I recall correctly, was also running for the US Senate. Indiana law requires major party candidates for US Senate to gather at least 4,500 valid petition signatures, but a minimum of 500 must come from each of the state's nine congressional districts.[126] Nonparty and minor-party candidates, meanwhile, had to gather petition nomination signatures equal to two percent of the total votes cast in the last Indiana secretary of state election, which at the time was in 2014.[127] With a total of over 1.3 million votes cast for that office in that election, that meant these independent candidates needed more than 13,000 signatures.

Ballot Access

Candidates for any political office do not just go to a Supervisor of Elections office to ask to be on a ballot when voting happens. There is a process that they must go through. Ballot access laws are set by each individual state, even for federal candidates. Therefore, the requirements for getting on the ballot will be inherently different depending on which state you are in, although they tend to look similar. Still, there are two main ways in which a prospective election candidate can appear on the ballot: gather a minimum number of petition signatures from eligible electors (i.e., registered voters who can vote on the office in question) and/or pay an application filing fee.

For higher-level or well-financed state legislative and local candidates, the application fee is merely pocket change. They are plenty of funds to pull from without a second thought, and it saves the time of painstakingly gathering petition signatures. The number of petition signatures needed and the filing fee not only vary from state to state but by type of office as well. The higher the level of office, the more signatures needed and the higher the filing fee. For *most* Republicans or Democrats who are serious candidates, these will not be a problem.

Yet if you are a nonparty candidate, it is consistently much harder to qualify, and not necessarily because they naturally have a harder time getting signatures or having the money to pay a filing fee. Conveniently, the ballot access rules are almost always different for third-party and nonparty candidates. Oftentimes (for nonparty candidates, at least), there is *no* option to pay a filing fee, and there are far more signatures required. Those Indiana and Texas examples mentioned at the beginning of the chapter are perfect examples.

There is also another major obstacle with the petition signatures, one that Republican, Democratic, and independent candidates must all face. Whenever a large batch of signatures are handed to election officials (e.g., county supervisors of elections), a few of them will inevitably be invalidated for all sorts of reasons. Let us say you hand in a stack of one hundred signatures at one time; you can usually expect something like seventy-five to ninety of them to get approved. Not getting approved may or may not be the fault of the people who signed the petitions. The reasons for invalidation can be anything from the voter not listening to how they had to be a registered voter in that district, the street address they put down (one of the personal bits of information they need to add to verify their voter registration data) may differ from what is on file, or the computers that sometimes process the signatures decided that a few of the signatures looked just a *little bit* too different from what is on file. Those are just a few reasons.

I can tell you from personal experience: gathering petition signatures is a frustrating, arduous process and not just because of the validation issues. You must usually go to public functions (e.g., county or state fairs) or other public areas where you sometimes need clearance to do campaign activity. Then you must convince people coming by to sign those petitions, sometimes needing to explain to them why you need the signatures. They could have all sorts of reasons for not wanting to sign your petitions, some of which have nothing to do with who or what you are gathering signatures for.

You also must make sure that they are a registered voter in the candidate's district you are gathering the signatures for. You must do all this only to have some of them dismissed as invalid. You may be surprised at how long all that takes if you have not done it before. Now account for the fact that nonparty candidates must get many more signatures than Republicans and Democrats do, and it becomes even more problematic.

"Official" Third Parties

A major hindrance for third parties in getting on the ballot deals with whether they are deemed an "official" party in a state. Not every third party is recognized in an "official" capacity in each state. It is a big deal for third parties to be recognized because it enables them to officially run a candidate under that party label in an election. While the Libertarian, Green, and Constitution Parties are the largest third parties in the country, not every state recognizes them as a label that a voter can register under or that a candidate can run as. As of the 2020 general election, the Libertarian Party had an official state affiliate party in thirty-five states, the Green Party was in twenty-two states, and the Constitution Party was in fifteen states.[128]

Each state has its own criteria for how to become a "recognized" party, although the basic process is roughly the same across states: a certain number of signatures from registered voters must be obtained, validated by a state's department of elections and/or county supervisors of elections. For example, Arizona's 2020 requirement for achieving the status of recognition was 31,686 valid signatures of registered voters.[129] The number needed will likely increase for 2022 as there will likely be more registered voters in the state; the total number of a state's registered voters is usually the biggest factor in the number of signatures needed. The criteria for party recognition may therefore be too high a threshold for some third parties to reach.

Some third parties are wholly unique to certain states. Vermont has the Vermont Progressive Party, California has the Peace and Freedom Party, Alaska has the Alaskan Independence Party, and so on. States might even have another category for those parties actively seeking an "official" status. Alaska, a state with a penchant for quirky state and local politics that do not simply divide neatly along Democratic and Republican Party lines, currently has *ten* such groups, including Libertarian, Green, and Constitution.[130]

Even if a party is not officially recognized by a state, that does not mean that a voter cannot register under such a label. That is why you can find a lot of different affiliations in a state when there are much fewer parties that can be explicitly noted on a ballot. The aforementioned political groups in Alaska are a good illustration. (You may have already found throughout this book that Alaska is a useful example for many talking points regarding independent politics.)

Campaign Finance and the Power of Independent Expenditures

Perhaps few aspects of campaigns are decried as much as the obscene amounts of money spent every year. Regardless of opinions on relevant laws, campaign finance rules have a lot of restrictions. Contributions *directly* made to a campaign have a limit, depending on who is making the contribution, which state the campaign is being held in, and what level of office is being sought (e.g., local judge, state representative, US Senate). There are all sorts of other stipulations that campaigns have to abide by regarding campaign finance.

Recent years, however, have seen the rise of what are called independent expenditures. These differ from regular campaign contributions in that they are not *directly* spent by a campaign, merely expressly in support of or against one— and these expenditures are unlimited, unlike normal contributions. However, it is highly illegal for organizations that dole out these expenditures to collaborate with a campaign in any way, shape, or form. They have sole control over how the money is spent and who they pay the money to, but they are separate from the campaigns themselves. The campaigns never see the money or have anything to do with its spending. That is what makes them *independent* expenditures, and such expenses are the major driving force beyond the obscene, skyrocketing amounts of money being spent in elections. Since independent expenditures cannot communicate with the campaigns they support at all, they can have differing messages.

Yet independent expenditures—perhaps ironically, given their name—are rarely made for or against independent candidates, parties, or their campaigns. This is a serious blow to most of their chances at higher levels of political office. Their voices are drowned out by independent expenditures advocating and opposing the Democratic and Republican candidates, the ads never even giving a hint that there is a non-major party candidate in the race. Independent expenditures, however, are much less common at lower levels of office, which might contribute to independent candidates' relative successes in local and certain state legislative races— even if only slightly.

The Unique Issues of the Presidential Race

The Electoral College debate was thrust back into the spotlight following the 2016 presidential election, where Hillary Clinton won a substantially higher number of *popular* votes, but Donald Trump decisively won the *Electoral College* vote. It was not the first time that the Electoral College system generated controversy, however.

There were several previous instances where the presidential election victor also did not win the popular vote.

- 1824 election: John Quincy Adams won following the "Corrupt Bargain of 1824," in which he conspired with Henry Clay.

- 1876 election: Rutherford B. Hayes won following the Compromise of 1877, where Democrats agreed to award Hayes the victory in exchange for Republicans ending Reconstruction in the South.

- 1888 election: Benjamin Harrison won following accusations of corrupt tactics such as vote buying, though the level of corruption and who is responsible is debated among scholars.[131]

- 2000 election: George W. Bush won following bitter battles in both the Florida Supreme Court and the US Supreme Court due to controversy over Florida's vote.

After Trump's victory in 2016, there was a renewed push to change the electoral system to a direct election, decided purely by a popular vote. Whether this is right or wrong is not the point here. This chapter will not focus on the debate—it is simply to set the stage for why the Electoral College makes it difficult for an independent to win. To illustrate why, we are going to pose a hypothetical situation.

Say that a third candidate does take a substantial number of Electoral College votes away from both the Republican and the Democratic candidates. You need 270 electoral votes to win, which is just over 50 percent of the total. An independent candidate captures enough that it is basically impossible that anyone will secure 270 or more votes. If no one gets that majority, the election is then decided by the US House of Representatives. There would be a handful of independent representatives in the chamber, at best. Democrats and Republicans are likely going to vote the party line because there is too much at stake. Thus, independents are still going to be out of luck.

Would an independent have a better chance of winning if the election were purely decided by a popular vote? It is possible but not definite. On the one hand, despite a few aberrations, the Electoral College split usually follows the popular vote split, and many voters would still likely worry about "wasting" their vote in a direct election. On the other hand, perhaps some voters would be more inclined to vote because they feel like their choice matters now, and that it didn't in the Electoral College system. There are plenty more arguments that could go either way.

Regardless, for the purposes of this discussion, those arguments do not matter because the Electoral College is what we have now. It is also only part of the puzzle. An independent candidate must get to the point where they are even an option for voters in the first place. This brings us back to the problem of ballot access.

Remember that the states individually decide their requirements to be on a ballot, and independents already have trouble with them in general. Yet most of them only need to concern themselves with one state's rules. The independent candidate for *president*, however, must qualify for each individual state's ballot if they want to maximize their potential votes. Republicans and Democrats also must go through a process to be on each state's ballot, but it is significantly easier for them to do so. They will always be on every state's ballot, even in states they have no chance of winning. It is already hard enough for an independent to get on one state's ballot for president, and it becomes exponentially more so when they have to do that for multiple states' presidential ballots.

It is not *required* for a presidential candidate to appear on all fifty states' ballots. In fact, most independents do not. For example, 2016 candidate Evan McMullin only appeared on eleven states' ballots as a listed option, was relegated to a write-in option on thirty-one states' ballots, and was not an option at all in eight states, according to Ballotpedia.[132] Those eleven states did not provide even remotely close to the 270 electoral votes he would have needed to win and stave off the US House of Representatives from deciding the winner. (He didn't win any states, anyway.) Regardless of other issues they face, independent candidates obviously cannot win if they are not an option in the first place.

Two's Company, Three's a Crowd

The Republican and Democratic Parties, being staples of American politics, are duking it out in almost every election. (Depending on what type of election and where it is, it might be an intraparty battle). In an increasing number of cases, however, the Republican or the Democratic Parties will have such a monumental advantage in a district that the other party will not even bother to run a candidate. If a candidate still runs, the party will give them a bare minimum boost, if anything. Most political operatives consider it a waste of resources to try to help a candidate who has absolutely no chance of winning.

Occasionally, a third-party or nonparty candidate will seize this opportunity to go up against only one major party nominee. They *potentially* have a better shot here because they only have to worry about messaging against one party, are less likely to get their voice drowned out during the campaign, and do not have the stigma of the disadvantaged major party label. On the surface, the logic makes sense, and it sometimes makes sense in practice too. Yet each district's unique circumstances and who the independent candidates are need to be factored in.

It generally becomes much harder for an independent candidate who must go up against both a Republican and a Democrat. Unless it is an extraordinary circumstance, the most either party's nominee will have to worry about is that independent candidate siphoning off just enough of their would-be supporters. Even when they do not mean to, or they object to the term, the independent sometimes plays the role political observers often call the "spoiler." The Republican and Democratic nominees will not have to craft a campaign plan against the third option the same way they would have to against each other, but they are still wary.

Meanwhile, the independent will have to convince moderates from both the Republican and Democratic Parties to support their campaign instead—and as we have seen in the voter behavior chapter, that is a monumental task. For all their gripes about their respective parties, those same moderates may be too fearful of what would happen if the "enemy" won the election.

If it is just a two-way race, however, it might be a prime opportunity for an independent candidate to contend for the seat by virtue of taking the place of one of the main parties. An independent may be more palatable to some voters than that main party that decided to sit out that race. Theoretically, at least, the independent can potentially grab the voters from that missing party and moderates from the participating main party. Of course, there are still a lot of factors that need to be considered, like how the voters in the district typically swing. Yet if we consider all else equal (even though that never really happens in politics), a two-way race is probably going to be a better chance for independent candidates than a three-way race.

Getting Heard

When primaries are over, and general elections start approaching, it is extraordinarily rare that you see more than two people on a debate stage: the Republican nominee and the Democratic nominee. If you are a more casual observer of politics, or sometimes even if you lean more toward "political junkie," you may be inclined to think that that is it and there is no one else competing in that election. Sometimes, that is definitively true.

However, looks can be deceiving. In many cases where there is a third opponent, whether they are a third-party or nonparty, and there is a debate being held, they are a no-show. It is not because they did not want to be there or they forgot about it. Those organizing the debate have set some qualification(s) that the third candidate needs to attain to be considered. Usually, this is done through polling—that is, a candidate must reach a certain level of support in polling. For the biggest elections, this often means an average from multiple news outlets' polls, such as CNN, NBC, ABC, CBS, and/or Fox News.

Independent candidates seldom meet these requirements. While Ross Perot did participate in presidential debates in the 1992 cycle, the Commission on Presidential Debates

(CPD)—established by both the national Republican and Democratic Parties in 1987—instituted the requirement for average support of 15 percent from five organizations' polling as selected by the CPD in 2000. So far, no independent (third-party and nonparty) has ever crossed the threshold since the first televised presidential debate featuring the candidates in 1960, not even Ross Perot.[133] (Technically, the first televised presidential debate was in 1956, but candidates Adlai Stevenson and incumbent Dwight Eisenhower did not participate. Former first lady Eleanor Roosevelt and US Senator Margaret Chase Smith of Maine acted as their surrogates, making it particularly noteworthy that the first televised presidential debate was between two women.)[134] For the congressional and lower-level elections, thresholds for participation by independents may depend on location and who handles organizing the debates.

An independent may get through the ballot access stage and even make some decent gains in campaigning for voter support. Yet if they cannot even be heard by a wide audience, there is no chance for them to gain real traction. A debate would by no means guarantee a real momentum shift in an independent candidate's favor, but it certainly is more beneficial than not being on the stage at all. The fact that there would at least be a chance at getting electoral momentum means getting on a debate stage would be critical for independents. (There will be more on this in the following chapter and how this contributes to a self-fulfilling prophecy that independents are perceived as "wasted" votes.)

Summary

It is already difficult enough to contend with campaign realities that are simply a natural part of politics, such as having to target likely voters. Obstacles that are baked into the system and not inherent to it make the slog that much tougher. Even getting on the ballot in the first place can be a daunting challenge and can derail candidacies before they even begin. Many of the rules and laws are written to deliberately thwart attempts from outside the Republican and Democratic Parties to even compete for a seat.

Despite how much independent candidates may cry foul about these issues, though, not much has been done. Even when they are heard, they are often quickly forgotten or dismissed. As with the matters regarding the election debate stage, much of the problem for independents lies in how much—or rather, how little—attention they receive. As you will see in the next chapter, it is not just the media and politicians with a vested interest that are responsible.

Chapter 9

Attention Paid to Independent Candidates

Independents have a problem with getting the spotlight on them—and being portrayed positively when they do.

Former Republican Governor of New Mexico Gary Johnson won the Libertarian Party's nomination for the 2016 presidential election. Libertarians are typically the main third-party contender in elections, being the most common third party in the country. For some of the race, Johnson made a fair bit of noise in the news for an independent (if your definition of independent also includes third parties). He was gaining enough traction in polling that there was some speculation that he would reach the criteria that allowed him to participate in a presidential debate: an average of 15 percent support from voters from five national polling organizations, as chosen by the Commission on Presidential Debates.[135]

Though the media, polls, and supporters may have hinted at it, however, Johnson was not really that close. Sure, he broke into two-digit levels of support on multiple occasions from July through September 2016.[136] [137] [138] Averaging 15 percent across five different polling organizations, though? Johnson still had a long way to go. He would not break through in time for the first debate and would effectively fade away, capturing only 3.3 percent of the popular vote in the election.[139]

When Johnson was in the news, however, it was often for the worst moments, even before the first presidential debate. Perhaps the most striking instance came from his response regarding a question about Aleppo. Aleppo is a major city in Syria and was one of the epicenters of the ongoing Syrian Civil War (as of June 2021). The city saw colossal damage and bloodshed in the lead-up to the 2016 US presidential election. In an interview where he was asked about what he would do regarding Aleppo, Johnson asked "What is Aleppo?" to the incredulous host of the show he was on.

While his campaign responded to the ensuing heavy criticism by saying he "blanked," it would not be the only gaffe Johnson committed. Other blunders when answering questions on TV helped to sink him, though they were far from the only reasons his campaign faltered. The story of his 2016 campaign displays how powerful and influential getting attention is for campaigns—especially for any independents. It is not just the media or the candidates themselves that play a big role, either. Academics, pollsters, and voters themselves also play key roles in how much attention, or lack thereof, is paid to independent candidates.

The 24/7 News World

Our senses are incessantly bombarded with the news, and never-ending campaign ads are thrown into the mix when elections are approaching. Campaigns are shelling out mind-boggling amounts of money, and they are only getting more and more expensive. While some other countries have a short, fixed period in which political candidates are allowed to officially campaign, there is no such hard limit in the United States. Whether it's publicly declaring candidacy, filing the official paperwork to be a candidate, teasing an announcement of running for office, or simply discussing candidacy with party operatives, jumping into the race for president a full year before the election is often considered far too late an entry. Even before major candidates declare their candidacy for open seats, news outlets tend to repeatedly talk about the "Will they or won't they?" side of the story. It gives them something to talk about, and there are plenty of interested viewers and listeners to consume it.

With this nonstop press, who are the people most talked about in the media regarding politics? They are Democrats and Republicans. Whether you lament this reality or not, it makes a lot of sense. While the public may say they are constantly tired of political talk, the bitterness of politics, and so on, their usual media consumption habits suggest otherwise. This relationship between the media and the public is perhaps the most critical in analyzing how the attention paid to independent candidates plays such a big role in those candidates' successes—and failures.

The Reciprocal Relationship Between the Media and the Public

Media market realities are also stacked up against independents. Before we get to that, though, we need to take a brief overall look at how much the media landscape has changed in the past five years or so. In the earliest days of TV, the only channels available were ABC, NBC, and CBS. Local newspapers, radio stations, and some magazines made up almost all the rest of the options for news. Plenty of newsrooms were well-staffed, well-paid, and experienced enough to consistently deliver high-quality, in-depth news pieces, with much less regard for catering to specific audiences.

Over the past forty to fifty years, the number of outlets vying for attention has skyrocketed. The sources dealing with political news and commentary have exponentially increased, and that's not even considering all the other entertainment-focused outlets that have exploded, nor the rise of social media. Changes in the media landscape have arguably hit local newspapers the hardest as they get continually gobbled up by big media corporations. Newsroom employment for newspapers has plummeted since around 1990, and between 1995 and 2015, the workforce was cut in half. Total newspaper ad revenue, both digital and print, dropped by more than half between 2005 and 2014.[140] [141] While in much better shape than local newspapers, network evening news ratings have fallen by more than half between 1980 and 2005.[142]

Now the media has become so fragmented, the echo chambers so narrowed, that many outlets *must* cater (some might say pander) to their audience. Pew Research Center shows that liberals and conservatives have greatly diverging views on what news sources are trustworthy.[143] Sometimes, the media actively encourages conflict in politics to boost ratings.[144] For all the media's flaws and the complaints made about it, the issue is not all on them. They are largely responding to what various segments of the general population want.

Independents, quite frankly, are not a sexy news splash the way Capitol Hill drama, the countless Republican versus Democratic battles, intraparty squabbles, or presidential news is. This is the case to an even greater extent with news becoming more nationalized (i.e., a hyper focus on national politics and scrutinizing state and local elections in the context of national politics). Citizens' lamentations of the toxicity of political media coverage and general discourse compete with the fact that conflict is interesting to us. Sometimes, it feels like all that media does is cover dissension and fighting. Much of how political conflicts play out is determined by how involved the audience gets in those conflicts, as seen in how conflict boosts ratings.[145]

Not everyone, however, seeks the news, and many actively try to avoid it, even frequent voters. With the seemingly endless number of TV channels, radio stations, websites, and so on that do not deal with politics, it is much easier for some people to tune out from the news. These people also infrequently vote, if at all.[146] Given their lack of attachment to politics, perhaps they might be more likely to vote for independent candidates (though that is not necessarily the case). When they do seek the news, however, they tend to find biased news outlets as these are the most readily available and well-known. So, if independent candidates rarely get coverage in the news already—at least, positive coverage and/or coverage of how they could be competitive with the two main parties—and would-be supporters only sporadically vote and watch the news, these independent candidates are hard-pressed to compete with their major party opponents.

Attention from the Media

The market focus does occasionally go to these independents, though. Every so often throughout a presidential election cycle, an independent might get hyped up, especially someone famous, whether they have teased a potential candidacy or not. Dwayne "The Rock" Johnson has been a popular proposal by some of the public since at least the 2016 election, but he has yet to hint at a run for office or truly dismiss it. A better example would be Howard Schultz. Schultz toyed with running for president in 2020 but fizzled out well before an actual declaration.

The hype for an independent is almost always built up long before a declaration is or would have been made, but the hot topic of the week in politics can change very quickly. Momentum can shift quickly in a campaign cycle, such as when Bernie Sanders and Pete Buttigieg jumped out to early leads in the 2020 Democratic presidential campaign only for Joe Biden to shoot past them later. With so many other competing news topics and so much media crowding for our attention, the independent candidate can easily get lost in the noise. They already have no margin for error as it is.

Even when an independent candidate is covered, oftentimes, the context is not what such a candidate wants. Here are two ways the media can destroy an independent's campaign: (over)publicizing blunders and labeling them as spoilers.

Stumbles are often much more detrimental to independent candidates than they are to Republicans and Democrats, such as Libertarian nominee Gary Johnson's "What is Aleppo?" comment during the 2016 presidential cycle. With so many voters being casual observers of politics, this likely is the only exposure they get to independent candidates, and they are turned off by the candidates as a result. It may be the only exposure for voters that are *more* tuned into politics, for that matter. The perception of independents having no chance at winning and being a "wasted vote" then persists.

Some independent candidates are considered "spoilers." Spoiler candidates are labeled that because, while considering an independent candidacy, they are known to normally lean either Republican or Democratic and would possibly "steal" votes from that major party's candidate, leading to victory for the opposing major party. They might have an above-average involvement in politics, such as donating to campaigns or endorsing candidates. The media pounces on these aspects, and the context immediately shifts to an independent being a "spoiler"—much to that candidate's chagrin. The discussion then becomes how many voters would siphon off their normal party's nominee, and that party then does whatever it can to dissuade that independent from running, or the tank that candidacy as soon as possible. Therefore, it is often not someone who is completely outside of the two-party system, but rather someone who is disgruntled to some degree with their party, enough that they seriously consider launching an outside bid for the office. For example, Howard Schultz was a potential independent candidate for president in 2020, but he was known as a Democrat.

Good or bad coverage, there is relatively little reporting on independent candidates in the thick of the campaign cycle. The focus is almost exclusively on the intraparty jockeying and then the Republican versus Democratic angle.

Those are what most of the public cares more about, including many of those same voters who are open to an independent candidate. We also often like having specific people to pay attention to because they become the embodiment of our values, at least from our perspective. Someone else could see them as completely antithetical to those values. Whatever the viewpoint, the leaders of the Republican and Democratic Parties are made much more obvious by the media.

Independent voters, on the other hand, have few key figures to turn to. For most voters, ideas of what independents are and who represents them are nebulous in comparison. The hard-core third-party voters, like some Libertarians or Greens, may get hyped up over their nominees, but there are so relatively few of them that they are only a blip in the overall voting population, rarely catching serious media attention. There is sometimes even less to focus on for candidates and voters who do not affiliate with any party. There are rarely any clear leaders that a wide swath of voters can point to and say, "That's who embodies that third party," or "That's who embodies independents." Ross Perot in 1992 was arguably a rare exception but by no means the rule.

Another prime opportunity for independent candidates to raise their recognition amongst voters would be in election debates, but as noted in the previous chapter, they seldom get that chance. Debate organizers dictate a certain threshold of support in voting is needed for independent candidates to participate. Yet how can they hope to achieve the necessary level of support if they are not even getting covered in the news? Then it becomes a cycle: independents cannot garner publicity, not enough people even know who they are, let alone support them, they miss out on debates and other chances at media exposure, rinse and repeat.

Attention from Academics

Academic studies are not at all devoid of any scholarly interest in independents. It is just that they are still often a footnote, or comparisons are made to them in the context of Republican versus Democrat. It is uncommon that they are the main event, but there are some exceptions.

By and large, however, studies do not often take a deep dive into what makes independent voters, candidates, and party officials "tick" beyond a couple of angles, and the ones that do are few and far between. If there are few to no academic articles, studies from think tanks, or original reporting from news outlets focused on this subject, obviously, there will be little to nothing for media pundits to talk about. Some consumers might be interested in these but will not be able to get them or know where to look for them. Independent campaigns could even use the studies to some extent to help their general strategy too.

When it comes to any sort of academic studies and articles (not just those pertaining to political science), the media coverage tends to crudely distill the findings into their most basic essences. Almost none of the nooks and crannies get mentioned, when the published studies themselves often have a section detailing their shortcomings and what future studies can expand on. The details bog down news segments that are already pressed for time and must hold the attention of news consumers. One might joke that virtually every food or drink can cause cancer because it seems that every study finds some way to identify that link, but the little nuances as to why are never given the time of day. So, even when media outlets report on these things, you will not get the full story because they must keep enough people's attention.

Still, some of the issue for independents lies with the

scholars themselves. The people that conduct these studies, regardless of how knowledgeable or well-resourced they are, have limited time, money, and mental energy to expend, so studies cannot truly cover everything they want to. Other scholars have even criticized previous studies for how they study independents, such as how they are defined and measured.[147]

Quite often, however, it seems their academic interests do not lie in studying the politics of independents. That might be a simple matter of what they find interesting to work on, but sometimes, it is a more personal motive. Whether they come from scholarly journals, think tanks, or elsewhere, some academics have a slant as to what they want to cover and may even receive funding from special interests and others who have a political agenda. These can also influence *how* they study the topic, raising the potential of confirmation bias, even though such studies are ostensibly unbiased. That goes for any kind of study into politics.

Academic studies are also meant to build on top of previous research. That is part of why you will often see giant blocks of text in reference sections showing what the study's author(s) used for guidance. The studies on Republicans and Democrats have continuously stacked on each other, while this has happened much less so for independents in part because there is much less previous research on them to draw from. Then you must account for how various third-party and nonparty voters and candidates are often lumped together into one giant conglomeration of "independents," when subgroups within are not necessarily going to think or act similarly to each other. This sometimes gets treated as a sidenote or is completely glossed over because a study is predominantly concerned with the two main parties.

Attention from Pollsters

The media and the public can't get enough of polls. The media need things to talk about, and the public has an insatiable curiosity for the "horse race" aspect of elections. The polling industry has received more intense scrutiny over roughly the past decade following a series of high-profile debacles, especially the 2016 presidential election. Despite ostensibly more people writing off polls as nonsense, they still get plenty of coverage and will continue to do so indefinitely. People still want to know what they have to say and often cling to polling results that say what they want to hear.

Some of the criticism pollsters have gotten is deserved—but a lot of it is not. Polling gets written off completely by some people because most of them do not understand how they work. A quality poll is extraordinarily hard to make. It takes a lot of time, money, people, and effort to do so—even more so the longer a poll is (e.g., the more questions are asked). There are critical considerations such as how to sample, the sample size, the number of questions to ask, and what topics to ask about. I would argue the biggest problem comes from the *interpretations* of polls. Media often does not look beyond the surface level of data (though if they did, it would not hold many voters' attention), and they miss key detailed data points that greatly impact the poll results.

Another issue is that not all polls are created equal—not even close. Most times in media, a poll is a poll, and therefore, it is newsworthy. Some polls are poorly made or made by non-reputable pollsters. A poll might even be completely fake, made by nonexistent pollsters simply to influence public opinion or troll people, such as the poll claiming that musician Kid Rock was leading US Senator Debbie Stabenow in her bid for re-election in the 2018 election.[148] Even if there are other issues with a poll—such as a sample size or the sampling method—it rarely matters to a media outlet. It makes for a story, which gets clicks/views/listens and money for them. Most of the public does not know the difference between good and bad polls, so it is an easy choice for the media to make.

The whole point of a poll is to survey a small proportion of the population because it is not feasible to get everyone's opinion. Their very nature means there is a small chance that their predictions can be in error. By and large, quality polling is solidly accurate. It is just the ones that are wrong that can get media coverage ad nauseum after being discredited.

So, where do independents fit in this? Oftentimes, the independent candidate(s) will not even appear in the poll. If that is the case, the media and/or the public will largely assume there isn't a candidate when there is. These independents might be otherwise credible candidates (or what some pundits might call "electable").

Poll results can and have influenced some voters' choices. If there is a perception that it will be a landslide, some of the losing candidate's supporters will not even show up. This happens a lot for these independent candidates, in turn becoming a self-fulfilling prophecy. After all, many voters feel a vote for an independent is "wasting" it and/or that the Republican and Democratic candidates are so objectionable that they feel there is no use in casting a ballot. If they do show up, voters may pick their second choice even if they don't really like the candidate, because they want to prevent the third candidate that they cannot tolerate from winning— an observation often labeled "strategic voting" or "sophisticated voting."[149] [150] Some other voters just want to be on the winning side and will vote for who they think will win—a phenomenon called the "bandwagon effect."[151] [152] [153]

If an independent *is* accounted for in a poll, that does not necessarily mean something good. If the pollster is employed by a Republican or Democratic campaign, they might only include them to see if there are any persuadable voters or normally loyal voters threatening to vote for a third choice. The rest of the poll might barely acknowledge that there is an independent. Regardless of how much focus independents get, pollsters and campaigns will make press releases that omit anything that can paint their own candidate in a bad light.

There is another way that independents get shortchanged when it comes to polls: commissioning polls themselves. As stated before, good polling takes a substantial investment of time, money, effort, and people who know what they are doing. Most independent campaigns have little to none of these. For the cheapest and most local seats (e.g., certain state house districts), this is much less of a conundrum because all the campaigns involved are not going to spend a ton of money. If it is a highly sought-after seat (e.g., US Senate), however, it becomes a serious issue.

This problem manifests itself in several ways.

- Independents have less access to reputable pollsters than the Republican and Democratic Parties. Many polling firms work only for one side or the other, or they will jump back and forth for campaigns that have the means to pay them well. Independents often do not get past the political view litmus test nor possess the funds in their coffers to pay the best polling firms.

- The most well-funded Republican and Democratic

campaigns can poll voters repeatedly. They will eat the cost if they feel they need the public opinion data. Even when an independent campaign can pay for a poll, they cannot do it often. Thus, being strategic in when the poll is commissioned is even more important for independents.

- Polls are often the best way for campaigns to get a better sense of how they should craft their campaign message—which voters they need to target, what different groups of voters' top issues are priorities, etc. Republicans and Democrats already have a bit of basic intuition about these elements from the get-go due to who their voter bases typically are, and polling helps refine the campaign strategy. Independents, on the other hand, have a much tougher time identifying any of these things without the help of polls if they do not have the means to commission a poll.

If you are an independent candidate or campaign organization and you cannot poll people, you are going in mostly blind. Republicans and Democrats at least have some tried-and-true demographics of voters that they can go for, but independents will have far fewer clues as to which voters are there for the taking. Independents also tend to have fewer connections to community leaders who know what the key issues are, and they do not have an obvious voter base to tap into, at least not like Republicans and Democrats do. An inability to poll effectively and accurately becomes another obstruction that independent candidates must go up against.

Summary

When looking at how the attention paid to independents affects their chances at winning offices, it is natural to look at it just in terms of the media's direct role. After all, they are supposed to be the ones informing the public, acting as "gatekeepers" of information. Just about everything flows through the media to get the public's attention.

However, that glosses over and minimizes the roles that other sources play. Candidates and organizations are sometimes not skilled or resourced enough to garner enough positive press. Voters may say they want more viable independents, but they also are usually far more interested in the usual Republican versus Democratic and intraparty news. Academics only occasionally dive into studying independents when there is a myriad of works pertaining to Republicans and/or Democrats. Pollsters give little focus or completely disregard independent candidates, and these candidates have much less access to robust polling.

Independent candidates and organizations certainly have their work cut out for them. Reading the book up to this point, it can be easy to be discouraged if you are someone itching for more officeholders outside the two major parties. While that was not the purpose, it is necessary to have a broad understanding of why it is so monumentally difficult for these independents to win elections, be they part of a third party or no party at all. Yet as you will see in these final chapters, not all is bleak for independents and their sympathizers.

Chapter 10

What Independents Have Going for Them

Independents have a lot of obstacles to overcome, but not everything is dire for them. Up until now, this book mostly focused on the impediments in their way because most people are not aware of them, and despite increasing complaints about both the Republican and Democratic Parties, they still thoroughly dominate American politics. There are still some silver linings, even if some are only slight advantages in comparison. Fully tapping into what gives them an edge is not going to suddenly lead to a deluge of independent victories across the United States—there are still plenty of blockades they must break down—but it can start improving results for them.

Voters' Openness to Independent Candidates

While the statistic may often be overblown by independent campaigns and organizations, the fact that there are regularly so many people open to voting for independent candidates is a start. Even when they are not necessarily likely to vote for an independent candidate, voters might still have a neutral or possibly even favorable opinion of them as indicated by polling. Usually, the independent candidate's name recognition will be low. While name recognition is critical to have, lower rates can give those candidates some opportunity to make an appeal to possible supporters' votes. (It will still be hard to gain that name recognition, though, as independent candidates still tend to be much more limited on funds and connections to people through which they can gain that recognition.)

While many Republicans and Democrats would never even consider voting for the opposing party, there are not nearly as many that outright oppose independents. It is more so the fact that they are too busy supporting their own party in an attempt to thwart the opposition rather than writing off a third option. The problem then shifts from "these voters will never support this candidate because they are fundamentally opposed to him/her" to "these voters would think about choosing the independent, but they are too focused on stopping the opposition from winning, and the independent will not be able to do that." The latter is still a huge blockade for independents to overcome, but it is a much better problem to have than the former.

It can also be harder to pin a highly negative label on independent candidates the same way participants in politics may do for Republicans and Democrats, though I would argue this is much more so the case for nonparty candidates than those for third parties. Third-party candidates sometimes have a stigma attached to their own party label. Some voters might see Libertarians as "head-in-the-sand isolationists" or think of the Greens as "tree huggers and hippies." They come across as goofy, in over their heads, uninformed, etc. The relatively few times people get media exposure to third parties often reinforce these perceptions, such as Gary Johnson's "What is Aleppo?" gaffe.

Those candidates who run as no party whatsoever are less likely to have such comparisons made about them because there is likely to be no clear label attached to them from the outset. Some voters may see all Libertarians as a group of Gary Johnsons or Ron Pauls, or all Greens as a group of Jill Steins. If those voters dismissed them as unserious candidates, they will probably see all their fellow Libertarians, Greens, etc., the same way. Still, many more voters are already going to have made up their minds about the Republican or Democratic Parties than those who have made up their minds about certain third parties.

What Ross Perot's 1992 Campaign Might Teach About Independents

Ross Perot's 1992 presidential campaign is arguably the most well-known independent campaign of recent memory. While he garnered no electoral votes, it is impressive that he managed to accumulate almost twenty million popular votes. While his campaign is not some blueprint to success, and the election landscape is vastly different from nearly three decades ago, there are some clear takeaways for independent political campaigns. Some of them might be able to be applied to nonpresidential races, even though their electoral circumstances vary greatly.

Remember how many voters that would potentially choose an independent do not do it because they do not want to "waste a vote"? Judging by the number of votes Perot received, there were clearly far fewer people that believed this. What was different about his campaign?

An academic study by political scientist and college professor Paul A. Beck perhaps shed some light on what one answer is. Although it is an oversimplified summary, the evidence from the study suggests that voters' support of Perot was more likely in a social context where there were more Perot supporters, even if the voters were Democrats or Republicans. In other words, the more Perot supporters a voter encountered and had political conversations with, the more likely that voter would choose Perot themselves. (However, partisans could "defect" to a major party if their discussion network had enough supporters of that major party's candidate.)[154]

Many people fear "wasting a vote" on a candidate they feel has no chance of winning, but if they perceive that that candidate's support is large enough, they can potentially be swayed to vote for that candidate. Of course, it is far from guaranteed that this would happen, and politics has gotten even more divisive since then. Yet independent candidates and operatives hoping to break down the walls of party preference can find some hope in the results of Beck's study.

As the media and the public are often far too focused on the national context of politics, it can seem like independent candidates never win elections. But as was noted in Chapter 6, they see more success when you get down to the state and local levels depending on where you look. Perhaps the results of Beck's study could be extrapolated and applied to some of those cases. It is hard to know for sure without clear evidence, but it is reasonable to think that these independents won, in part, due to voters' perception of large enough support for them.

Independent Election Victories

Independents can also point to current officeholders and recent victors from third parties and no party at all. According to the US Libertarian Party's website, there were 229 Libertarians in elected office as of August 11, 2021, with 99 of them in partisan offices and 130 of them in nonpartisan offices.[155] Even though those nonpartisan offices should come with an asterisk (given that the candidates' regular affiliations do not appear on the ballot and voters may have been blind), that still means something if you are an independent. According to the Green Party's elections database, 39 of their candidates won seats in 2019, and 19 candidates won seats in 2020.[156] [157] While almost all of those were very local candidates, and there may be some nonpartisan races there, you must start somewhere.

For those voters who want candidates that are completely nonparty, Bill Walker is the most notable recent example. (I do not use Bernie Sanders or Angus King here as they are known to caucus with the Democratic Party in the US Senate.) Walker won the governorship in Alaska in 2014, defeating the incumbent and member of Walker's former Party, Republican Sean Parnell, in a state that regularly leans red. Eliot Cutler came within a couple of percentage points of winning the governor's race in Maine in 2010, and that was with both a Republican and Democratic nominee in the race.[158] As for the state legislative level, there were five nonparty state senators and nineteen state house representatives as of June 16, 2021.[159]

More Opportunities for Independents to Win

Chapters 6, 7, and 8 had the heaviest focus on campaigns

themselves and demonstrated the various electoral scenarios available. While it is unusual for independents to win regardless of the type of election, some situations could lend themselves to more success. As noted in Chapter 6, some types of elections are potentially more beneficial to independents based on the type of primary held. Top-two and blanket primaries are theoretically the best options here. Independent candidates actually get to participate in these primaries, unlike in closed primaries. (Third-party candidates can only participate in closed or open primaries if a state has a third party that can hold primaries of their own, as noted in Chapter 6).

As concerning and dangerous as it can be to have decreasing numbers of uncompetitive seats—where one major party is so disadvantaged, they cannot possibly beat the other major party—it could create major opportunities for independents. An independent candidate can be the stand-in for the absent Democratic or Republican candidate while being a completely different kind of candidate. Theoretically, the independent can draw out the voters from the major party with no nominee while being potentially palatable to voters from the dominant major party who are disgruntled with their own candidate. Of course, that depends on just how dominant the participating party is, but there may be a few instances where the opportunity is there for an independent candidate.

While split-ticket voting has been on the decline, it does still happen, and areas where this happens could opportunities for independent candidates as well. Split-ticket voting refers to when a district's total vote goes to a major party candidate for one office, but the district supports a candidate from the other major party for a different seat. It is usually pointed out in the comparison between the presidential vote and a district's US House vote. For example, a US House district could have chosen its Democratic candidate while also picking a Republican for the presidency.

The reason areas that engage in split-ticket voting can be advantageous to independent candidates is that it suggests some ambivalence toward the two parties in those districts. If voters in these places can sway between parties, there may be a reasonable chance an independent can garner support here too. That ambivalence could drive ticket-splitting (at least for the president and Congress) in the first place.[160]

None of this guarantees success by any means. It does not confer even a moderate chance of success, taken on its own. I cannot stress enough in this book that every election, every race, and every district is different. They all have unique circumstances that need to be accounted for (even though you will still find some commonalities). However, this is meant to generate some thought processes and an understanding of how these elements can affect election outcomes.

Progress on the Ballot Access Front

Attempts to strike down ballot access laws restricting independent candidates have been met with mixed success. The courts are pretty much the only recourse left for them to go after these laws, with the occasional exception of citizen-proposed ballot measures in states where that is allowed. While there is still a long way for independents to go, every victory in court counts, and they have gained some major successes.

It seems that most often, independent political groups

challenge such laws based on the First Amendment and Fourteenth Amendment. There are five specific rights established in the First Amendment—religion, speech, press, assembly, and petition—but assembly and petition are the particular rights in question. The Fourteenth Amendment provides the Equal Protection Clause. Here are some major court cases and their rulings.

- *Bullock v. Carter* (1972): The US Supreme Court ruled in a 7–0 decision that Texas' primary filing fee system, which imposed costs as high as $8,900, violated the Fourteenth Amendment as it placed unequal weight on candidates and voters based on their ability to pay.[161] [162]

- *Lubin v. Panish* (1974): A somewhat similar situation to the *Bullock v. Carter* case, the US Supreme Court unanimously ruled that states cannot require lower-class candidates to pay filing fees they cannot afford, as this violates both the First and Fourteenth Amendments.[163] [164]

- *Storer v. Brown* (1974): In another case involving both the First and Fourteenth Amendments, the US Supreme Court in a 6–3 decision upheld a California law that prevented independent candidates from running for election if they were registered with a qualified political party during the year prior to the preceding primary election. However, it also ruled that requiring a number of petition signatures equal to five percent of eligible signers was likely unconstitutional.[165] [166]

- *Illinois State Board of Elections v. Socialist Workers Party* (1979): The US Supreme Court unanimously ruled that new political parties and independent candidates could not be required to gather more petition signatures for elections in a political subdivision such as a city or county (in this case, Chicago) than the number of signatures that would be required for statewide elections.[167] [168]

- *Anderson v. Celebrezze* (1983): In a close 5–4 decision, the US Supreme Court ruled that Ohio's early filing deadline for independent candidates to stand for election was unconstitutional on the grounds of both the First and Fourteenth Amendments.[169] [170] [171]

- *Norman v. Reed* (1992): In part a reaffirmation of the decision in *Illinois State Board of Elections v. Socialist Workers Party*, the US Supreme Court ruled in a 7–1 decision that Illinois violated the First Amendment by requiring third parties and their candidates to gather more than 25,000 petition signatures, the threshold for statewide office, to participate in elections for political subdivisions.[172] [173]

It is still an incredibly steep hill for independent candidates to climb when it comes to ballot access. There are still plenty of laws that make it more difficult for them to officially stand for election. Yet independents can take comfort in the fact that the highest court in the nation, the US Supreme Court, has broken down some of the barriers to their entry. Time will tell future developments, but it is likely the US Supreme Court will have to strike down more of these ballot access laws.

Other Potential Advantages

Admittedly, some other advantages become somewhat more speculative, but they are also potential boons to independents' cause. Independent organizations, inevitably, are getting better simply by gaining more experience, though they still make some of the same mistakes (e.g., focusing too heavily on people's surface-level frustrations with the two major parties without addressing the psychological blocks that keep most voters from voting for an independent). Some Republicans and/or Democrats might underestimate their independent opponents in the few cases an independent *does* have comparable chances of winning. Other plus-sides will depend on the specific election in question, as some races will naturally be a bit more likely to go to an independent candidate than others.

Summary

Independent candidates have a considerable amount of work cut out for them, but there's still hope for them. They have won some elections, however few they may be. They have won ballot access cases that went all the way up to the US Supreme Court, sometimes reversing a lower court decision—which is extraordinarily difficult, not just because it is the highest court in the nation but because they have an incredibly high threshold for what cases they are even willing to hear. Independent candidates and organizations need to fully harness any advantages they can without overestimating how much is on their side and underestimating what stands against them.

Speaking of which, the natural end to this discussion leads to what these independents could do to make themselves more viable in future elections. It may be the epitome of easier said than done, but many of these changes and more need to be made if independents want to be consistent contenders—a serious force to be reckoned with.

Chapter 11

How Independents Could Become More Viable in Elections

In the introduction of this book, I explicitly stated that this book is not meant to be some sort of step-by-step guide to independents winning more elections. Even if it was, it is impossible to guarantee success because of all the reasons in this book and more.

This chapter is probably the most subjective of all, as it gives some suggestions as to what can and should be done to make independents more competitive. There are no easy answers. Still, there are some general ideas about improving independent candidates' viability that can be made, and they relate to all the previous chapters. Independent organizations, regular voters wanting something different from Republicans or Democrats, and those simply just interested in political science will find some useful takeaways here. It should be noted that a lot of independent candidates and campaign operatives understand some of this already; however, there are still some things that have not been sufficiently considered, if at all, such as some of the risk-taking psychological studies.

To break through into the two-party system, you must weaken what makes the two-party system so strong in the first place. Independents have been trying, and sometimes succeeding, at making advancements here, but oftentimes, independent advocates think they are much closer to breaking through than they really are. Independents do not approach their predicament from every angle they should: it's not just about ballot access, running legitimate candidates, and gaining more resources to run better campaigns. There are many factors not being considered, mostly because the knowledge is not well-known. Focusing on all these elements is a necessity and will lead to better strategies and messages aimed at voters.

So, what are some ways that independents can become more viable and potentially successful at winning elections? It is significantly easier said than done, but here are some of the most critical elements based on the previous chapters. Buckle up because there is a lot to discuss.

Truly Understanding the Psychology of Self-Identified Independents

There are numerous ideas of what an "independent" is, but independents tend to receive a blanket description when they should not be treated as a uniform group at all. Not every independent is a moderate or centrist, as was demonstrated in Chapter 2.

Furthermore, discovering the profile of an independent voter requires understanding the profile of a Republican and a Democrat. You need to have baselines of the two main parties and what tends to separate the moderately partisan from the highly partisan. Demographics are a core part of this profile, but so are other things like values, priorities, and how they see labels like "Republican," "Democrat," or "independent."

The biggest psychological stumbling block of all is breaking the stranglehold of the "wasted vote" mentality. That mindset is partly a result of how much politics is portrayed as dichotomous. It's seen as one choice or the other—in this case, the only "viable" choices are Republican or Democrat.

Breaking True and False Dichotomies

Many of the issues for independents, at their core, stem from trouble with dichotomies. More specifically, it is a matter of what people's perceptions of dichotomies are. Some of them are real, yet many of them are false, propagated for personal political goals. Dichotomies, both true and false, are all the rage in politics. They have been for virtually the entire history of the United States as a free nation. What makes them so popular and effective?

For one thing, it makes for easy consumption by the audience. We naturally want things simplified, particularly if it is something unfamiliar to us. Sometimes, too many options overwhelm us—even if it is something as simple as deciding where to eat for dinner or something more complicated like a dataset for running advanced statistical measures. Debates in politics are commonly painted as a battle between good versus evil, establishment versus anti-establishment, complete support of a policy versus total opposition, red versus blue, and so on—with no middle ground.

Are things always that simple, though? Absolutely not. Here are some examples.

- "Evil" is a disturbingly overused word for things and people we disagree with, even if we vehemently disagree.

- There are more than two degrees of how much someone is part of the establishment (not to mention that the word is rarely clearly defined). Does "establishment" just mean being in office for a particular length of time, does it pertain to their voting record with the party, or is it something else?

- There are degrees of support and opposition to broad policy issues, even if it is as contentious as, say, abortion. As one person is pro-choice in every scenario while one person is pro-life in all of those, another person might only support it in cases where the mother's life is in danger and/or if the baby has a severe birth defect, for example. Many people fall somewhere in the middle ground, but the voices far on either side drown out the moderate voices.[174]

For another, when we are strongly invested in something, it is much easier to see things as an either-or choice. We have all been in the "my way or the highway" mentality at some point, though some people much more than others. Politicians, media, political commentators, activists, etc., try to appeal to our emotions to some degree because it works. It gets us to listen. There is nothing inherently wrong with those appeals—no matter how rational we think we are, we are all governed by our emotions to some extent. However, oftentimes in politics, these appeals become disingenuous and dangerous. They turn people against each other.

Still, there are many things in politics that really are simply an either-or choice. Oftentimes, there really are only two choices to pick from for an elected office, without even a write-in option. A vote on a bill boils down to a yes or no. A policy might be specific enough—narrowly affecting one small area or group of people and/or making one highly particular change—that it truly is a dichotomous decision.

If you cannot break the dichotomy of "the lesser of two evils," your independent campaigns will not matter. You can spend a ton of money. You can raise your name recognition. You can even get on a debate stage to gain some more momentum. But if you do not convince people that there is a legitimate contender other than a Republican or Democrat in the race, someone who can change politics for the better, all that effort will be for nothing.

Increasing Ballot Access

Obviously, winning more elections requires getting on the ballot in the first place, but Chapter 8 shows roadblocks there too. Becoming more competitive, then, requires changes to ballot access laws, which are in the domain of state legislatures—even when it comes to federal elections.

Early in the nation's history, the political parties supplied ballots, not state governments. (Really, what could have *possibly* gone wrong there?) While the Republicans and Democrats were still clearly the dominant forces, third parties were regularly able to grab some elected offices, even in Congress. A series of Progressive reforms in the late 1800s and early 1900s shifted this power over ballot access to the state governments. As their legislatures were always run by either Republicans or Democrats (or split between them), the states gradually snuffed out the influence and power of third parties, chiefly through dramatically increasing the number of petition signatures necessary to appear on the ballot.[175]

Chapter 10 demonstrated some progress that independents have made in ballot access since then, yet there are still substantial roadblocks ahead. For example, even though the US Supreme Court struck down certain petition signature requirement laws such as in *Illinois State Board of Elections v. Socialist Workers Party* (1979) and *Norman v. Reed* (1992), there are still high signature thresholds that severely hamper independent candidates, sometimes making it almost impossible for them to appear on the ballot.

While it is a good thing that the parties no longer supply ballots, independents need to find a way to break down these exorbitant signature requirements to more equal levels with Republican and Democratic candidates. The increased thresholds are clearly a substantial reason for the lack of competitiveness from independent candidates. Probably the only effective way to address this is through the courts, as has been done previously. As with those previous court cases, the First and Fourteenth Amendments are two of the most potent weapons against these ballot access rules. Depending on the state, there may be some state constitutional laws or statutes that can be harnessed as well.

Changes to Polling

Part of the problem is an overreliance on public opinion data showing 1) a large proportion of voters calling themselves "independents" and 2) a large proportion of voters saying they would consider an independent candidate. On the surface, it might sound like the two-party system is on the verge of crumbling, but that is a misinterpretation of the data.

- As discussed in Chapter 2, people call themselves "independent" for all sorts of reasons. A centrist independent—the kind that is usually thought of most when talking about an independent candidate—is not going to be voted for by independents who think that either the Republican or Democratic Party are not far enough to one ideological side.

- Oftentimes, the survey questions ask people if they are "open" or would "consider" voting for a third-party or nonparty candidate. That is far different from the "likelihood" of voting for an independent. Not everyone open to voting for an independent has the same likelihood of doing it.

- The questions do not explore what would make people vote for an independent or what they want most out of an independent.

As was noted in Chapter 9, good polling is incredibly difficult to do. Open-ended questions—ones where the respondent can give any answer they want—are much more in-depth than multiple choice questions or questions that rank on a number scale. However, open-ended questions are also more expensive, take more time to ask and answer, and are harder to analyze.

Independents have more problems to contend with when it comes to polling than the two major parties: there are far fewer pollsters that are available; there is generally far less money at their disposal to pay for more robust, in-depth polls; and the pollsters that are available to independents, *overall*, do not have the level of experience that Republican and Democratic pollsters do. Thus, independents must choose even more wisely than their partisan counterparts what they ask and how they ask it. Benefactors may have to financially contribute even more to independent political operations.

Still, there are some potential ways for independent candidates, operatives, and benefactors to address the issue. The questions asked in independent polls need a shake-up. Do not just ask if a poll respondent identifies as an independent but why they identify as an independent. Do not just ask if the respondent is open to, or considering, voting for an independent, but gauge the likelihood that they would do so. You might gauge that likelihood by using a numeric point scale. Dig deeper into what would make a voter cast a ballot for an independent candidate. For many of these voters, disappointment or anger directed at the two major parties is not enough. Otherwise, a lot more of them would vote for a third option more often.

Those in-depth solutions do come with drawbacks, mostly to do with feasibility issues. They would need more questions, more frequent polling, and more open-ended questions. All those make polls more expensive and difficult to analyze. Here are a couple of examples of analysis issues.

- If someone rates their likelihood of voting for an independent at sixty points out of one hundred, do you target their vote similarly to someone who rated their likelihood at fifty points, or seventy-five points? A one-hundred-point scale is more in-depth, but analysis can get too cluttered. There is little difference between, say, thirty-four and thirty-six out of one hundred.

- If you ask someone what makes them an independent, how do you group responses according to similarity? Is "I don't like the two parties" close enough to "I want something different because of the excessive partisanship"? What if somebody has multiple answers in one, such as "I can't stand the excessive partisanship, they rig the system, and they do not share my values"? You cannot easily group these answers.

On the one hand, you get more clarity, better information with which to strategize, and respondents might feel like they are being heard when they previously were not. On the other hand, it makes things more complicated, more expensive, and harder to sift through. Like many things in politics, there are trade-offs.

Election Process Reforms

Clearly, the election process itself—specifically, when an independent is campaigning for office and/or already on the ballot for election—is slanted against independents too. The solutions that would make independents more competitive are not obvious. Consider Unite America's campaign reforms they are advocating and putting resources into. (Note that in these cases, they support candidates from both the Republican and Democratic Parties that are supportive of these changes.) They list four of these on their website: independent redistricting commissions, ranked-choice voting, nonpartisan primaries, and the expansion of vote-by-mail.[176] Whether these are worthy endeavors or not, there should be some skepticism as to whether they really will lead to greater competition outside of the Republican and Democratic Parties.

Redistricting commissions. How about independent redistricting commissions? There are thirty-three states where their legislatures have the authority to redraw congressional district lines and thirty-three states (though not all the same ones) where they can redraw their own state legislative boundaries. The state legislative district lines are *not* the same as the congressional district lines. The other states either use separate commissions or a hybrid that incorporates input by both separate commissions and the state legislatures.[177]

Still, it is not a straightforward fix. Some of these separate commissions do not allow their members to hold political office.[178] That might seem like it cuts out partisan interests, but just because they do not hold political office does not inherently mean the commission will be nonpartisan. The members can still have ulterior partisan and ideological motives; they may even run for office in the future when the district lines are set (unless there are rules against this). How do we account for this? How do we verify they are not coordinating with partisan or ideological interests?

Even if redistricting really is balanced between Republicans and Democrats, what about all the third-party and nonparty voters? They are not unified in how they define "independent," as Chapter 2 showed. Are they going to be divided into districts in a way where different kinds of independent candidates have a realistic shot at winning elections? Can you even realistically consider this in redistricting? If you are looking for a centrist independent, they might get too diffused with the independents who want a more hardline candidate outside of the major parties. Can you even gerrymander third parties when each party tends to have fewer members? There are a lot of questions to ask that are rarely brought up—or at least seem to be rare. Truly independent redistricting commissions are essential to level the playing field because elected officials have repeatedly demonstrated a willingness to rig redistricting in their favor when possible.

Ranked-choice voting. What about ranked-choice voting (RCV), as discussed in Chapter 6? It certainly holds some promise. RCV, open primaries, top-two, and blanket primaries would give independent candidates better chances at winning elections than closed primaries do. In the case of RCV, however, it remains to be seen just *how much* it increases their chances due to not enough data. At the very least, I believe closed primaries need to be substantially phased out if independent candidates are to have better opportunities at winning elections.

Nonpartisan primaries. What about nonpartisan primaries? They are nominally nonpartisan, but functionally, they are not necessarily as nonpartisan as you may think.[179] Exhibit A would be Nebraska, the only state legislature that is both unicameral (meaning one chamber in the legislature) and uses nonpartisan elections. In reality, most of Nebraska's state senators are affiliated with a party, as can be seen from endorsements, member lists directly provided by the state Republican and Democratic Parties, and senators' voter registration data.[180]

Vote-by-mail. What about vote-by-mail (VBM)? The COVID-19 pandemic has, in part, propelled this policy to the forefront when talking about election reform. As of June 2021, seven states—Colorado, Hawaii, Nevada, Oregon, Utah, Vermont, and Washington—had all-mail voting elections where every voter receives a mailed ballot without the need for voters to request one, though not all are *exclusively* vote-by-mail.[181] Among the arguments made in favor of the expansion of vote-by-mail is that it will increase voter turnout, save taxpayer money by reducing costs of elections, make elections more secure, and make voting more accessible for more people.[182] It is true that it leads to more accessibility, simply by default; every voter gets a ballot mailed to them without needing to request one. Research on Colorado's VBM suggests that it does save money.[183] Whether it makes elections more secure is out of the purview of this writing.

Does VBM lead to increased turnout, however? That is debatable. A study by political scientist Adam J. Berinsky suggests that it not only leads to little if any increase in turnout, but that these reforms are more likely to be used by those who are already more likely to vote anyway (e.g., politically engaged, higher educated, higher income people).[184] This could be particularly problematic for independents, as they are in greater need of higher turnout. They rarely can pull enough support from the people that are showing up to vote, as evidenced in part by the few times they do win elections.

This demonstrates, once again, that a significant part of the issue is voter engagement, as Berinsky points out. You can make voting as easy as you want, but if people do not care or they endemically feel that their choice does not matter, they are not going to cast a ballot.

Proponents sometimes argue that it will help voters better memorize their choices and more effectively use technology to make informed choices.[185] VBM may allow for that, but that does not necessarily mean that it *will* happen. Voters still must be engaged enough to want to put in that effort to research. Even when they do or they want to, some candidates are difficult to research, particularly many independent candidates. Voters must know where to look, and those candidates must make information about them somehow available; sometimes, they do not even have so much as a campaign website. VBM, on its own, will not spur a serious increase in turnout, lead to better researching of the candidates, or even more votes for independents.

There are other reforms that might help, too, such as the expansion of multi-member district usage and the implementation of proportional representation. MMDs give more opportunities for independent candidates to win seats. Proportional representation would give independent candidates at least a little reward for winning a proportion of the vote. These wouldn't necessarily give them a *significant* boost in representation, but it would be more than what they have now.

Better Strategies

The Republican and Democratic Parties have been around for a considerably long time. They have the financial means, connections, infrastructure, and electoral benefits at their disposal to be seemingly everywhere in politics. But even they cannot participate in every single election there is. With a trend of decreasing competition in congressional, state legislative, and even some local area elections, it makes no sense for them to try.

Some independent candidates and campaigners try to compete in elections they have absolutely no shot at. They sometimes try to follow a similar basic formula to Republicans and Democrats although independent campaigns are and must be fundamentally different. Certainly, some considerations are the same: you must know which voters are predisposed to support an independent candidate, which voters are potentially persuadable, what media realities affect voter outreach, etc.

However, some independent candidates and organizations assume the general malaise regarding the two major parties means they have a chance to win in more elections than they really do. There are very different concerns at the local level than in the country at large, even if there are some similarities. If an independent cannot persuade voters that they understand those local issues, let alone that they are a viable candidate, they will not win.

Therefore, exponentially better strategies and better intuition about viability in elections are vital even for credible independent candidates. Here are some of the biggest considerations.

- What is the makeup of the electorate, especially in terms of party affiliation? That is assuming that this information is available, as not every state keeps track of party affiliation. Even when they do track party affiliation, each state varies in what other demographic data they provide.

- Look at the history of the district or state you are running in, especially in similar types of election years. That will give you some idea of how this race could turn out. For example, if you are running for election in a presidential election year, and your office had an election in the last presidential election year, that could provide some guidance. If you were running in 2020, looking at how 2016 shaped up for your district is highly important.

- You cannot go in blind, hoping to raise enough money while fundraising to contend. While you cannot predict everything during a campaign, you need an estimate of how much the campaign will cost and if you can raise the funds necessary. If the Republican and/or Democrat is spending millions of dollars and an independent candidate can only raise something like $80,000, do not even bother running.

- Make a physical campaign plan. See Chapter 7 concerning campaign plans.

- Consider starting small. Some independents want to get ahead of themselves and go straight for the big leagues, but something as local as city council or county commission may be a better way to go. It will help you build up connections, name recognition, experience, and more for when you want to run for higher offices. Not to mention that local offices tend to have the most direct impact on people's day-to-day lives.

- If you find that there is no chance for you to win an election, consider not running and instead pitching in support for independent candidates elsewhere and persuading your supporters to do the same. Independent candidates need all the support they can get.

Better Infrastructure

The campaign infrastructure for independents—perhaps especially for nonparty candidates—is nowhere near as robust as those for the Republican and Democratic Parties.

The major parties are in every county in the United States. There is an abundance of College Republicans, College Democrats, and grassroots organizations that volunteer for the major parties.

State affiliates. While the Libertarian, Green, and Constitution Parties have numerous state affiliates, a lot of states still don't officially recognize them as a party, they do not have remotely close to the level of resources that the state-level Republican and Democratic Parties do, and there are a lot of localities that do not have their own third-party affiliate. On the nonparty front, Unite America is arguably even more hard-pressed. They do not have many state and local affiliates, although they have been expanding recently.

Micro-targeting. Another major advantage that the major parties have is a robust database on their voters. These databases contain an immense amount of information, sometimes provided by those voters themselves. They sometimes even contain data that, at first glance, may seem like they have nothing to do with politics. Seemingly apolitical bumper stickers, lawn decorations, magazine subscriptions, and more can clue the major parties into voters' political views and how they are likely to vote. As crazy as it may sound, these provide a fair amount of accuracy because voters from each party have some commonalities in what they read, what they slap on their car bumpers, etc.

Independents are probably not going to be able to attain such level of detail. Even if they did, it would be much harder to gauge how persuadable they are in supporting independent candidates. If they have not already created such a database or invested much into one, it should be a strong consideration. These databases help the Republican and Democratic Parties to "micro-target" voters, meaning they can more directly appeal to individual voters instead of only large swaths of them at a time.

Micro-targeting is probably even more critical for independents in figuring out just who can be brought to their side or which voters can be turned out to vote at all. Republicans and Democrats at least tend to have certain demographic groups more predisposed to voting for one of them, but that is highly difficult to gauge for independents. Thus, mass appeals may not work out well unless you have deeper, individual-level data.

Community. Another way to build up infrastructure is to create an accessible community for independents, especially for those who do not belong to a party. In Chapter 10, I noted a study that might help explain why Ross Perot was such a relatively successful candidate despite being an extremely distant third-place finisher. There were "discussion networks" where, if voters encountered Perot supporters more often and had more discussions with them, they were more likely to vote for Perot.[186]

While that was only one election that the study looked at, the results hold some promise for independent candidates and campaigners. Part of the reason why some voters feel voting for an independent is a "waste" is how they perceive the numbers of Republican and Democratic voters. If people thought there were many more independent supporters, that might persuade them to feel that voting for a third option is not so useless.

What would this look like? Social media like a Facebook community, Reddit subreddit, or Discord channel may have some benefit, but not everybody uses those, and those that do may not know where to look for these kinds of communities. Even so, the "discussion networks" already on those sites and apps are nothing even close to what would be necessary for independent candidates and campaigns to become a serious force to be reckoned with. Another potential option could be a messaging or social networking app where like-minded independents, and people open to independent candidates, can communicate. There would have to be a lot more to it than simple messaging, however. Educational aspects such as information about what various independent movements are, the candidates that are running as independents, and more could be added.

Better Candidates and Building for the Long Run

There is a tendency for independents—candidates, campaign operatives, advocates, voters, and even sympathizers from the Republican and Democratic Parties—to be short-sighted. They focus too much on the big splashes like winning high-profile races or touting seemingly favorable polling results. That is not a problem in and of itself, but aiming too high and in too many places can be detrimental to what you are trying to do.

Experience and connections. Oftentimes, Democratic and Republican officeholders in Congress and the presidency have had experience holding lower-level offices or in public policy or advocacy. It is a similar case with state legislators, with some of them having county- or city-level seats. Of course, that is not always the case, but it certainly helps much of the time because they have built up the connections and political networks necessary to attaining most public offices.

Independent candidates, on the other hand, do not have that kind of experience and personal ties as regularly as their major party counterparts. Independents who are in that boat should consider going for the most local-level elected offices more often, so they can build up their experience and connections.

To truly have a considerable impact in politics, there needs to be less short-sightedness and more looking toward the long-term. Even the Republican and Democratic Parties must build up these "benches" of talent, as discussed in Chapter 7. That means it is even more important for independent groups to do so.

Likability. Especially in higher-level elections (like Congress) or state executives (like a governor), independent candidates need to be spectacular at many facets of campaigning to have even a decent chance at winning. The Democratic and Republican Parties put too many resources into these elections for just any independent to compete, let alone win. They may be a credible and "electable" candidate, but they cannot be a force to be reckoned with if they do not exceed in various personal and political traits.

These qualities do not necessarily involve political views. Independent candidates need to stand out in other ways to get the attention and support they need to compete. Ross Perot had some of these characteristics, which arguably contributed to his strong showing (for an independent candidate) in the 1992 presidential election. Whether you liked him or not, he had charisma in spades, and while certainly not every elected official has that, an independent will need to be especially magnetic to get media attention and overtake the major party candidates.

Money and fundraising. Perot also had a ton of his own money as a businessman. Money is not the end-all-be-all— Donald Trump defeated Hillary Clinton despite being outraised and outspent by a nearly two-to-one margin, according to Bloomberg News data.[187] Independent candidates, however, cannot compete financially if they cannot back up their own campaign with a substantial amount of personal funds.

But even that money will mean nothing if the independent candidate cannot fundraise. Even if they could bankroll their campaign, they would be accused of attempting to "buy the election." Fundraising also means forging relationships with people who have the connections to garner support for the independent's candidacy. These networks matter even more for independent candidates than for Republicans and Democrats, who also often have a built-in party infrastructure to tap into.

These are some of the most important traits independent candidates need. They need to be utterly unique to win these big-time offices. Otherwise, there is no chance that enough would-be voters would gravitate to them.

A Unified Purpose: No Party or a Third Party?

One of the most fundamental issues for independents is… well, what exactly is an independent? That is why Chapter 2, which tackled that very question, was so early in the book. You cannot make significant strides in independent representation in government if you do not have a clear vision of what an independent is. To make independents more viable in elections, you must address this question in some way.

For the purposes of this book, I defined an "independent" in Chapter 1 as simply anyone who is neither a Republican nor a Democrat. When I discussed a specific kind of independent, I denoted it with terms such as third-party, nonparty, centrist independent, and so on. But that is the problem: there are too many kinds of independents under that general term. They all pull in different directions because their goals and policy views are not the same.

Third-party or nonparty candidate designations each have their own advantages, but they both have faults with long-term sustainment. The current third parties, even the largest ones—the Libertarian, Green, and Constitution Parties—have low levels of membership and are often looked down upon as goofy. However, there is nothing to really clue you in on what a nonparty candidate believes by virtue of having no party label. As noted in Chapter 4, everybody uses heuristics and symbolism to make sense of complicated things. However misused and abused such concepts can be for someone's political agenda, they are necessary.

Chapter 4 also noted issues with collective action. To really move toward and achieve common goals, there must be a unified structure for large groups of people, but large groups are also highly difficult to organize well. Organized groups will beat unorganized groups almost every single time.[188] [189] That is especially the case for parties, which provide those opportunities to achieve common goals.[190] While nonparty candidates can win a few elected offices here and there, those independents that genuinely want to shake up the two-party system need something to unite behind. Unite America is, by far, the most organized group for nonparty candidates to seek assistance from, but they are still far too small an organization to go toe-to-toe with the Republican and Democratic Parties consistently.

The only way that can happen long-term on a large scale is for one third party to rise above the rest. Unite America is not exactly its own party (though perhaps they are considering it in the future), but they would be critical to any chance at a legitimate third party. At least one party is trying to fill that hole in the middle of the political spectrum: the Serve America Movement (SAM). As of June 2021, SAM was either registered, or attempting to register, as an official party in Connecticut, New York, Pennsylvania, and Texas.[191]

Maybe SAM will become that third party that many Americans have said they want to compete with the two major parties, but they will need a lot more firepower than they currently have. That will require uniting more like-minded independents to their cause, such as Unite America. If the centrist-independent movement wants to have a chance at fundamentally changing politics as we know it, they cannot stay fractured in too many groups pulling in different directions. The independent movement needs to be organized for a common purpose to regularly compete with the big kids on the block.

Summary

This may be a lot to take in, but it is necessary for understanding the work ahead for these independent candidates and organizations and what stands against them. Many political observers know they have a lot of difficulties competing, but they often do not realize just how much that is the case. This is no step-by-step guide of how to be competitive as independents; however, if you are looking to make candidates much more viable in elections, changes in all these facets and more are critical—polling, ballot access, voter psychology (perhaps the most insufficiently accounted for aspect), building an infrastructure, better campaign strategies, and so on.

That just leaves some final thoughts on my part to wrap this all up. What does the future hold for independent candidates? That becomes mostly speculation at this point, but it is worth talking about. We will also confront what is probably the foremost question on the minds of those who read this book: Can an independent candidate (third-party or nonparty) ever win the presidency of the United States?

Conclusion

If you are hoping for a centrist-independent movement to become its own, it is probably easy to look at all these chapters and be discouraged. However, the silver lining for you is that now you are far more aware of the reasons why independent candidates are so hard-pressed to win elections. A confluence of factors combines to keep their success rates abysmally low. Breaking down most of those walls is necessary if you want to start reversing independent candidates' election outcomes—particularly if you are a centrist independent.

Can Centrist Independents Bridge the Divides in This Country?

While the extent to which American politics is polarized is debatable, the fact that we *are* polarized is not. There is an exceptional amount of bitterness, anger, and hate in discourse today, amplified by the media and those who benefit from the dissension. But the good news is that it is not an insurmountable gap. To some extent, we perceive polarization to be more pervasive than it actually is because of how much the media and partisan/ideological elites focus on it and highlight the most extreme views.[192] [193] This "false polarization" is particularly noticeable when the most politically active people on one side of the spectrum are evaluating and categorizing the beliefs of the other side.[194] [195]

Independents, particularly those who are centrist, subsequently get lost in all this noise. The polarization can make it seem like there is little middle ground; but that middle ground does exist. The polarization can be mitigated to some extent. When people learn what the real average views of the opposition are, ones that are not as extreme as expected, they may moderate their own opinions as a result.[196] In some cases, extreme views are a result of one's overconfidence in what they understand of policies, and when made aware of how little they comprehend that policy, they can moderate their own views.[197]

This is critical information for centrist independent candidates and operatives to capitalize on. These candidates tend to need a considerable proportion of both Republican and Democratic support in their campaigns, given that independent voters vote at lower rates and they are a diverse bunch with different conceptions of what they want in an independent candidate anyway. Educating these voters about what the opposition more likely believes and the nuances of policies and policymaking holds promise for future successes by centrist independent candidates and campaign professionals.

All this warrants revisiting the debate between Alan Abramowitz and Morris Fiorina as to whether American politics is really polarized, as discussed in Chapter 2. Abramowitz explains there has been a trend toward uniformity in how the parties are composed in racial, geographical, ideological, and cultural contexts. There are also important variations within the parties on specific issues, with polarization and sorting occurring on some issues and not others.[198] [199] Fiorina says that elites and voters who are more partisan or ideological are highly polarized and not representative of the overall voting population. Yet the former disproportionately affect politics compared to those less-invested, so being unrepresentative of the overall population does not matter much if the more politically oriented are the ones making all the decisions.

The Big Question: Can an Independent Win the Presidency?

Of course, this question is probably the preeminent question for most people reading this. The presidency is usually the context spoken of when it comes to speculation about independent candidates winning elections. The short answer is "not anytime soon." But this warrants a revisit of the Electoral College versus direct election debate. (Again, this is not a normative debate about which one is the "right" system.)

Since the Electoral College is what we have now, that will be addressed first. Chapter 8 showed some of why the Electoral College makes it particularly difficult for an independent to win. To claim the presidency outright, a presidential candidate needs to capture at least 270 of the Electoral College's 538 total votes, the minimum for a majority. There is no way that an independent candidate can muster that, even if they thwart the Republican and Democratic candidates in their own quests to win. It does not matter whether they are a third-party or nonparty candidate.

If no candidate reached that 270-vote threshold, the election then falls to the decision of the US House of Representatives. It is virtually guaranteed that each member of the chamber would simply choose their party's candidate. Even if a few "true" independents were in office at that time and subsequently picked the primary independent candidate, they would still be dwarfed by the numbers of both partisan sides. The moderate Republicans and Democrats are likely not going to risk incurring the wrath of their parties' strongly partisan elements, especially when either the Republican or Democrat is clearly going to win the presidency. Thus, the vote would simply go to the party with the most members in the US House.

The only way for independents to thwart that, then, is to go from the ground up. They must build toward winning the highest office in the land, which requires at least much of what was described in Chapter 11. Independent organizations and candidates often do not look at the long term sufficiently, trying to catch too many big breakthroughs in the short term. (To their credit, however, many of them are getting better about this.) Since the presidential election would inevitably go to the US House if an independent candidate were to capture enough electoral votes, there needs to be a substantial number of US House Representatives that are "true" independents. Even then, they will still likely need some moderate Republicans and Democrats to agree to join them in voting for the independent presidential candidate, and that is extremely difficult to do with what's at stake. In any case, independent candidates need to climb up through the ranks over time to make this scenario even remotely plausible. Now, what if the push for having voters directly elect the president (i.e., the winner simply needs the most popular votes to win) were to gain more steam and become a reality? Forget whether that is realistic for now and think about it hypothetically. Would an independent presidential candidate have a better chance to win in a direct election than through the Electoral College? You might be inclined to believe so, but that is highly debatable. There are still so many cards stacked against them. It would be a minimal change, if any, in how problematic these issues are for independents. While there have been major exceptions, the Electoral College vote still roughly follows the popular vote in most cases. Even if the presidential winner needs a simple plurality of the vote, the voting habits of most people are not going to suddenly change. Ballot access laws are still a serious roadblock. Independents still need to run much better campaigns and have the resources at their disposal. The list goes on and on.

The Future Viability of Independent Candidates in General

In a broad sense, will we have a substantial rise in the number of independent candidates holding elected offices? I try to refrain from straightforward predictions too much, but it is certainly possible. It is, and will continue to be, a prolonged process. It requires many changes in the approach to politics from a lot of different sources: academics, media, candidates, organizations, advocates, pundits, sympathizers from the Republican and Democratic Parties, and—arguably most important of all—the voters.

Statistics are all the rage these days, and that especially seems to be the case in sports and politics. It makes sense: numbers are usually more concrete and straightforward estimates. We all like having assessments that are more simplified and set in stone, to some extent. Yet I cannot responsibly nor reasonably put forth a numerical prediction about the future of independent campaigns, if that is what you were hoping for. It is simply not possible to legitimately make such a prediction. But if independent voters, candidates, organizations, and advocates start sufficiently addressing the issues of Chapters 1 through 9 and taking the steps outlined in Chapter 11, there is hope for greater success for independents in the future.

Author Bio

 Paul Rader earned a BA from the University of South Florida in political science and an MA from the University of Florida in political campaigning. He has hands-on knowledge of the political process and both educational and professional experience with research and analysis on various facets of political science. These aspects include election trends, the function of campaigns, the history of political institutions, government structure, public policy, and more. Paul used information gleaned from academic and practical graduate school classes, his work for nonpartisan companies, an internship with a company involved in independent politics, and the study of politics in his free time to write this book. He is also a member of Pi Sigma Alpha, the National Political Science Honor Society.

Paul currently works as an assistant staff writer with Ballotpedia and a senior page editor with Sayfie Review, a political news aggregator for Florida politics. As a big believer in increasing civic and political awareness, you can also find him writing about political science in his spare time on his nonpartisan, nonideological blog on Medium.com.

Paul counts a variety of other interests beyond political science. Among his favorite hobbies are sports (particularly football and basketball), video games (an especially avid fan of The Elder Scrolls and Fallout series), astronomy, history, and making memes. Paul is also a proud Floridian, living in the state for all but the first four months of his life, though he can also joke at its expense.

Glossary

Ballot access	The rules and regulations dictating how candidates can officially become candidates in an election.
Ballot measure	Basically, a law that citizens can vote on to determine whether it becomes a reality. Each state has different thresholds for whether a ballot measure becomes law—some states, for example, require more than a simple majority of votes to pass.
Bandwagon effect	Describes actions by a voter who simply wants to be on the winning side and thus chooses which candidate they think will win the election.

Blanket ("jungle") primary	*This book* defines this primary election as similar to a top-two primary, but a candidate can win the whole election outright if they receive a majority of votes in the blanket primary. "Blanket primary" and "top-two primary" are often interchanged and are somewhat semantic, but this leads to confusion. Thus, this book makes the two types separate and explicitly defines the difference.
Centrist independent	An independent who is somewhere roughly in the middle on the ideological spectrum (i.e., they don't lean much to either the conservative or the liberal side).
Closed primary	A primary election where only voters registered with the party can vote in it. For example, a closed Republican Party primary only allows Republican voters to participate in it.
Constituency	Basically, the same thing as an electorate. See the definition for "electorate."
Electability	A nebulous term describing whether somebody has qualities that voters would reasonably vote for. There are no definitive criteria for this term.

Electorate	The body of voters for a given election. For example, the electorate for the seventh congressional district of Ohio consists of all registered voters that reside within Ohio's seventh congressional district boundaries. Basically, the same thing as a constituency.
General election	The election that decides who wins the seat(s) being voted on.
Gerrymander	The illegal and deliberate drawing of district boundaries to unfairly benefit one party and/or disadvantage another party.
Ideology	A system of ideas or beliefs that form someone's political outlook. Examples include "conservative" and "liberal."
Incumbent	The current occupant of an elected office.
Independent (general term)	While people's definitions of the term vary, *this book* defines it simply as anyone who is neither a Democrat nor Republican. Thus, it can describe a third party or somebody who does not affiliate with any party.
Independent Party	A specific third party. It is *not* required to be a member of this party to be considered independent, but some voters misunderstand this. An *Independence* Party also exists.

Lieutenant governor	The second-in-charge official of a state, behind the governor. Think of the governor as the "president" of the state, while the lieutenant governor is the "vice president" of the state.
Majority Coalition	Describes parties who have banded together to jointly rule a government by agreeing to a deal. These are exceptionally rare in the United States, appearing almost exclusively in countries whose political systems have three or more large parties. That is because, in these systems, a single party rarely will have enough seats in government to rule on its own.
Moderate	Means that somebody leans toward the conservative or liberal side of the ideological spectrum, but not heavily.
Multi-member districts (MMDs)	Electoral districts where more than one candidate wins a seat. For example, a state legislative district with four seats being voted on means that the four candidates with the most votes will win the election, each taking one of the seats.
Nationalized politics	Describes non-national politics that are being viewed through a national lens. State- and local-level elections have their own circumstances, but nationalizing them means they are being viewed in the context of national politics (e.g., does a county commission candidate support Donald Trump).

Nonpartisan primary	A primary where none of the candidates run explicitly as members of any party, even though their voter registration may be with a party. Only the candidates' names appear for that election. This does not, however, prevent political parties from getting involved in the election unless a state or local law specifically prohibits such action.
Nonparty (no party)	Describes someone (e.g., voter, candidate) that is not affiliated with any party at all.
"Official" state party	A party who is officially recognized in a state and can run candidates under that party label on election ballots. Each state has different guidelines for how a third party can become an "official" party. The Republican and Democratic Parties are the only two that are official parties in all fifty states and Washington, D.C.
Open primary	A primary election where a voter can choose which party's primary to vote in regardless of their own party affiliation.
Partisanship	Describes the party affiliation of someone (e.g., Republican, Democrat, Libertarian) and how strongly they support them.
Petition signatures	Signatures from voters that are required to officially place a candidate or something else (e.g., a ballot measure) on the ballot so that the person or thing can be voted on.

Primary election	A sort of "prelude" election to the "real" general election. Primary election winners advance to this general election.
Prisoner's Dilemma	A thought exercise that pits (usually) two people against each other to see whether they would help themselves or help each other in a predicament. Their actions determine how their reward or punishment.
Ranked-choice voting (RCV)	A type of election where voters rank the candidates in order of preference. If no candidate wins a majority of votes in the first round, voters' second-place choices are counted, and the candidate with the lowest number of votes in the first round is eliminated. This process is repeated in successive rounds if there is still no candidate that receives a majority of votes.
Redistricting commission	An organization set up to redraw congressional or state legislative district lines. Depending on state laws, these can feature elected officials or people outside of elected government.
Respondent	Someone who answers or responds to a survey/poll.

Semi-closed primary	A primary election where voters registered with the party AND voters not registered with any party can vote in it. Voters with a different party *cannot* vote in that first party's primary. For example, a Democratic Party semi-closed primary allows Democratic and nonparty voters to participate, but Republicans must participate in their own party's primary.
Semi-open primary	Similar to an open primary, but a voter must choose which party to register with to vote in that party's primary.
Single-member districts (SMDs)	Electoral districts where there is only one candidate that can represent it. The vast majority of districts in the United States are SMDs.
"Strategic voting"	Describes actions by a voter who thinks their first candidate preference has little to no chance of winning and thus votes for their second choice in an attempt to thwart the third, fourth, etc., choices from winning.
Third party	Any specific party that is not the Republican or Democratic Party. This includes the Libertarian, Green, and Constitution Parties.

"True" independent	Someone who is the kind of independent most people think of when they hear the term "independent." Most people assume that independents are middle-of-the-road in their political views when that is not necessarily the case. The quotation marks are there to avoid gatekeeping (i.e., arbitrarily dictating who has reason to call themselves independents) while still being descriptive.
Top-two primary	A primary election where all the candidates are on one list, and the top two vote-getters advance to the general election to face each other directly.

Want to learn more about the various aspects of political science? I curated a quick, free guide of informative resources covering voting by officeholders, news, the function of government, public policy, original analyses, and more!

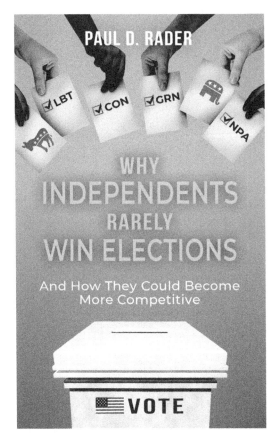

Get a copy by going to the following webpage:

https://bit.ly/wirweguide

Grab your free stuff today!

References

Chapter 1

1   "Political Independents: Who They Are, What They Think," Pew Research Center, March 14, 2019, https://www.pewresearch.org/politics/2019/03/14/political-independents-who-they-are-what-they-think/.

2   "Public Trust in Government: 1958-2021," Pew Research Center, May 17, 2021, https://www.pewresearch.org/politics/2021/05/17/public-trust-in-government-1958-2021/.

3   "Support for Third U.S. Political Party at High Point," Gallup, February 15, 2021, https://news.gallup.com/poll/329639/support-third-political-party-high-point.aspx.

4   "Public Trust in Government: 1958-2021."

5   "Government," Gallup, accessed June 20, 2021, https://news.gallup.com/poll/27286/government.aspx.

6   Richard E. Fenno, Jr. *Home Style: House Members in*

Their Districts (Boston: Little, Brown, 1978).

7   Christopher Ellis and James A. Stimson, *Ideology in America* (New York: Cambridge University Press, 2012).

Chapter 2

8   "Trends in Party Identification, 1939–2014," Pew Research Center, April 7, 2015, https://www.pewresearch. org/politics/interactives/party-id-trend/.

9   "Party Affiliation," Gallup, accessed July 16, 2021, https://news.gallup.com/poll/15370/party-affiliation.aspx.

10   "Registering By Party: Where the Democrats and Republicans Are Ahead," University of Virginia Center for Politics, July 12, 2018, https://centerforpolitics.org/crystal-ball/articles/registering-by-party-where-the-demo-crats-and-republicans-are-ahead/.

11   "Partisan Affiliations of Registered Voters," Ballotpe-dia, accessed June 20, 2021, https://ballotpedia.org/Parti-san_affiliations_of_registered_voters.

12   David B. Magleby and Candice Nelson, "Independent Leaners as Policy Partisans: An Examination of Party Identification and Policy Views," *The Forum* 10, no. 3 (2012).

13   Morris P. Fiorina, "America's Missing Moderates: Hiding in Plain Sight," *The American Interest* (March–April 2013).

14   Alan I. Abramowitz, *The Polarized Public? Why American Government Is So Dysfunctional* (New York: Pearson Education, 2013).

15   Pamela Johnston Conover and Stanley Feldman, "The Origins and Meaning of Liberal/Conservative Self-Identifications," *American Journal of Political Science*

25, no. 4 (1981): 617–645.

16   Philip E. Converse, "The Nature of Belief Systems in Mass Publics (1964)," *Critical Review* 18, no. 1/3, (2006): 1–74.

17   David E. RePass, "Searching for Voters along the Liberal-Conservative Continuum: The Infrequent Ideologue and the Missing Middle," *The Forum* 6, no. 2 (2008).

18   "Political Typology Reveals Deep Fissures on the Right and Left," Pew Research Center, October 24, 2017, https://www.pewresearch.org/politics/2017/10/24/political-typology-reveals-deep-fissures-on-the-right-and-left/.

19   Magleby and Nelson, "Independent Leaners as Policy Partisans."

20   "Political Independents: Who They Are, What They Think."

21   Samara Klar and Yanna Krupnikov, *Independent Politics: How American Disdain for Parties Leads to Political Inaction* (New York: Cambridge University Press, 2016).

22   Green Party US (website), accessed June 20, 2021, https://www.gp.org/.

23   "Ten Key Values," Green Party US (website), accessed June 20, 2021, https://www.gp.org/ten_key_values.

24   "Seven Principles," Constitution Party (website), accessed June 20, 2021, https://constitutionparty.com/principles/seven-principles/.

25   "Twelve Key Issues," Constitution Party (website), accessed June 20, 2021, https://constitutionparty.com/principles/twelve-key-issues/.

26   Arthur H. Miller and Martin P. Wattenberg, "Measuring Party Identification: Independent or No Party Preference?" *American Journal of Political Science* 27, no. 1 (1983): 107–108.

27   Miller and Wattenberg, "Measuring Party Identification," 107–108.

28   "Political Independents: Who They Are, What They Think."

29   Barry C. Burden, Bradley M. Jones, and Michael S. Kang, "Sore Loser Laws and Congressional Polarization," *Legislative Studies Quarterly* 39, no. 3 (2014): 305.

30   Abramowitz, *The Polarized Public?*

31   Alan I. Abramowitz and Kyle L. Saunders, "Is Polarization a Myth?" *The Journal of Politics* 70, no. 2 (2008): 542–555.

32   Alan I. Abramowitz, Brad Alexander, and Matthew Gunning, "Incumbency, Redistricting, and the Decline of Competition in US House Elections," *The Journal of Politics* 68, no. 1 (2006): 75–88.

33   Fiorina, "America's Missing Moderates."

34   "Trends in Party Identification, 1939–2014."

35   "Party Affiliation."

36   "Americans Continue to Embrace Political Independence," Gallup, January 7, 2019, https://news.gallup.com/poll/245801/americans-continue-embrace-political-independence.aspx.

37   Lydia Saad, "Americans' Political Ideology Held Steady in 2020," Gallup, January 11, 2021, https://news.gallup.com/poll/328367/americans-political-ideology-held-steady-2020.aspx.

38   Fiorina, "America's Missing Moderates."

39   Morris P. Fiorina, Samuel A. Abrams, and Jeremy C. Pope, "Polarization in the American Public: Misconceptions and Misreadings," *The Journal of Politics* 70, no. 2 (2008): 556–560.

40   V. O. Key, Jr., The Responsible Electorate: Rationality

in Presidential Voting 1936–1960, First Vintage Books ed. (New York: Vintage Books, 1966), 3.

Chapter 3

41   Congressional Quarterly, Inc., *Guide to US Elections*, 3rd ed. (Washington, DC: Congressional Quarterly, 1994), 263.

42   Congressional Quarterly, Inc., *Guide to US Elections*, 263.

43   Congressional Quarterly, Inc., *Guide to US Elections*, 263.

44   Congressional Quarterly, Inc., *Guide to US Elections*, 272.

45   Congressional Quarterly, Inc., *Guide to US Elections*, 268–269.

46   Congressional Quarterly, Inc., *Guide to US Elections*, 26.

47   Congressional Quarterly, Inc., *Guide to US Elections*, 260.

48   Congressional Quarterly, Inc., *Guide to US Elections*, 261.

49   "1912," The American Presidency Project (website), accessed July 14, 2021, https://www.presidency.ucsb.edu/statistics/elections/1912.

50   Congressional Quarterly, Inc., *Guide to US Elections*, 267.

51   Congressional Quarterly, Inc., Guide to US Elections, 271.

52   Congressional Quarterly, Inc., *Guide to US Elections*, 264.

53   John H. Aldrich, *Why Parties? A Second Look*, (Chicago: The University of Chicago Press, 2011): 103.

54   Aldrich, *Why Parties?* 103.

55   Joseph F. Stoltz III, "'It Taught our Enemies a Lesson': The Battle of New Orleans and the Republican Destruction of the Federalist Party," *Tennessee Historical Quarterly* 71, no. 2 (2012): 112–127.

56   Congressional Quarterly, Inc., *Guide to US Elections*, 263.

57   Congressional Quarterly, Inc., *Guide to US Elections*, 272.

58   John H. Aldrich, *Why Parties? A Second Look* (Chicago: The University of Chicago Press, 2011): 23.

59   "Political parties and leaders," CIA World Factbook (website), accessed June 21, 2021, https://www.cia.gov/the-world-factbook/field/political-parties-and-leaders/.

60   "Alaska House of Representatives elections, 2018," Ballotpedia, accessed June 21, 2021, https://ballotpedia.org/Alaska_House_of_Representatives_elections,_2018.

61   "Alaska House of Representatives elections, 2020," Ballotpedia, accessed June 21, 2021, https://ballotpedia.org/Alaska_House_of_Representatives_elections,_2020.

62   William H. Riker, "The Two-Party System and Duverger's Law: An Essay on the History of Political Science," *The American Political Science Review* 76, no. 4 (1982): 753–766.

63   John H. Aldrich, *Why Parties? A Second Look* (Chicago: The University of Chicago Press, 2011): 58.

64   Orit Kedar, Liran Harsgor, and Raz A. Sheinerman, "Are Voters Equal Under Proportional Representation?" *American Journal of Political Science* 60, no. 3 (2016): 676.

65   "State legislative chambers that use multi-member

districts," Ballotpedia, accessed June 21, 2021, https://
ballotpedia.org/State_legislative_chambers_that_use_
multi-member_districts.

Chapter 4

66   James N. Druckman and Rose McDermott, "Emotion and the Framing of Risky Choice," *Political Behavior* 30, no. 3 (2008): 297–321.

67   George A. Quattrone and Amos Tversky, "Contrasting Rational and Psychological Analyses of Political Science," *American Political Science Review* 82, no. 3 (1988): 719–736.

68   David L. Eckles, Cindy D. Kam, Cherie L. Maestas, and Brian F. Schaffner, "Risk Attitudes and the Incumbency Advantage," *Political Behavior* 36, no. 4 (2014): 731–749.

69   Larry M. Bartels, "Partisanship and Voting Behavior," *American Journal of Political Science* 44, no. 1 (2000): 35–50.

70   Larry M. Bartels, "Beyond the Running Tally: Partisan Bias in Political Perceptions," *Political Behavior* 24, no. 2 (2002): 117–150.

71   Patrick R. Miller and Pamela Johnston Conover, "Red and Blue States of Mind: Partisan Hostility and Voting in the United States," *Political Research Quarterly* 68, no. 2 (2015): 225–239.

72   Miller and Conover, "Red and Blue States of Mind," 225–239.

73   Steven Greene, "Social Identity Theory and Party Identification," *Social Science Quarterly* 85, no. 1 (2004): 136–151.

74   Richard R. Lau and David P. Redlawsk, "Advantages

and Disadvantages of Cognitive Heuristics in Political Decision Making," *American Journal of Political Science* 45, no. 4 (2001): 951–971.

75   Cindy D. Kam, "Who Toes the Party Line? Cues, Values, and Individual Differences," *Political Behavior* 27, no. 2 (2005): 163–182.

76   Wendy M. Rahn, "The Role of Partisan Stereotypes in Information Processing about Political Candidates," *American Journal of Political Science* 37, no. 2 (1993): 472–496.

77   Milton Lodge and Ruth Hamill, "A Partisan Schema for Political Information Processing," *The American Political Science Review* 80, no. 2 (1986): 505–520.

78   "Partisan Antipathy: More Intense, More Personal," Pew Research Center, October 10, 2019, https://www. pewresearch.org/politics/2019/10/10/partisan-antipathy-more-intense-more-personal/.

79   Saad, "Americans' Political Ideology Held Steady in 2020."

80   "In a Politically Polarized Era, Sharp Divides in Both Partisan Coalitions," Pew Research Center, December 17, 2019, https://www.pewresearch.org/politics/2019/12/17/in-a-politically-polarized-era-sharp-divides-in-both-partisan-coalitions/.

81   Mancur Olson, *The Logic of Collective Action: Public Goods and the Theory of Groups* (Cambridge: Harvard University Press, 1971).

82   Martin Gilens and Benjamin I. Page, "Testing Theories of American Politics: Elites, Interest Groups, and Average Citizens," *Perspectives on Politics* 12, no. 4 (2014): 564–581.

Chapter 5

83   "1992," The American Presidency Project, accessed July 14, 2021, https://www.presidency.ucsb.edu/statistics/elections/1992.

84   "1996," The American Presidency Project, accessed July 14, 2021, https://www.presidency.ucsb.edu/statistics/elections/1996.

85   "1912," The American Presidency Project.

86   "Minority and coalition control of state legislative chambers," Ballotpedia, accessed July 14, 2021, https://ballotpedia.org/Minority_and_coalition_control_of_state_legislative_chambers.

87   "Partisan Composition of State Legislatures," Ballotpedia, accessed August 16, 2021, https://ballotpedia.org/Partisan_composition_of_state_legislatures.

88   "Bill Walker (Alaska)," Ballotpedia, accessed July 15, 2021, https://ballotpedia.org/Bill_Walker_(Alaska).

89   Tegan Hanlon and Annie Zak, "Alaska Gov. Bill Walker ends campaign for re-election, backs Mark Begich," Anchorage Daily News, October 24, 2018, https://www.adn.com/politics/2018/10/19/gov-bill-walker-drops-out-of-campaign-for-alaska-governor/.

90   Andrew Kitchenman, "Nation's Only Independent Gov. Drops Re-Election Bid In Alaska And Backs Democrat," NPR, October 20, 2018, https://www.npr.org/2018/10/20/659136775/nation-s-only-independent-gov-drops-out-of-campaign.

91   "Maine gubernatorial election, 2010," Ballotpedia, accessed July 15, 2021, https://ballotpedia.org/Maine_gubernatorial_election,_2010.

92   "List of current mayors of the top 100 cities in the United States," Ballotpedia, accessed June 1, 2021, https://

ballotpedia.org/List_of_current_mayors_of_the_top_100_cities_in_the_United_States.

93   Tina Nguyen, "Howard Schultz Blames Back Surgery For Derailing His Campaign," Vanity Fair, June 12, 2019, https://www.vanityfair.com/news/2019/06/howard-schultz-suspends-2020-campaign.

Chapter 6

94   "Party Divisions of the House of Representatives, 1789 to Present," United States House of Representatives (website), accessed July 14, 2021, https://history.house.gov/Institution/Party-Divisions/Party-Divisions/.

95   "Party Divisions of the House of Representatives, 1789 to Present."

96   Michael J. Dubin, *Party Affiliations in the State Legislatures – A Year by Year Summary, 1796-2006* (Jefferson, NC: McFarland & Company, Inc., 2007).

97   "State legislative elections, 2020," Ballotpedia, accessed July 15, 2021, https://ballotpedia.org/State_legislative_elections,_2020. These stats were counted through the tabs under the subheader "Elections by state." Note that the one independent senator indicated under the Pennsylvania tab was not up for election in 2020. Thus, he was not counted in the total number of independent candidates who won an election.

98   "Nebraska State Senate partisan affiliation," Ballotpedia, accessed July 14, 2021, https://ballotpedia.org/Nebraska_State_Senate_partisan_affiliation.

99   Chris W. Bonneau and Damon M. Cann, "Party Identification and Vote Choice in Partisan and Nonpartisan Elections," *Political Behavior* 37, no. 1 (2015): 43–66.

100   "Primary election," Ballotpedia, accessed July 14, 2021, https://ballotpedia.org/Primary_election.

101   "Primary election."

102   "State Primary Election Types," National Conference of State Legislatures (website), accessed July 14, 2021, https://www.ncsl.org/research/elections-and-campaigns/primary-types.aspx.

103   "Alaska Ballot Measure 2, Top-Four Ranked-Choice Voting and Campaign Finance Laws Initiative (2020)," Ballotpedia, accessed July 14, 2021, https://ballotpedia.org/Alaska_Ballot_Measure_2,_Top-Four_Ranked-Choice_Voting_and_Campaign_Finance_Laws_Initiative_(2020).

104   Jessica Trounstine, "Evidence of a Local Incumbency Advantage," Legislative Studies Quarterly 36, no. 2 (2011): 255–280.

105   Alexander Fouirnaies and Andrew B. Hall, "The Financial Incumbency Advantage: Causes and Consequences," The Journal of Politics 76, no. 3 (2014): 711–724.

106   Gary W. Cox and Jonathan N. Katz, "Why Did the Incumbency Advantage in U.S. House Elections Grow?" American Journal of Political Science 40, no. 2 (1996): 478–497.

107   "Ranked-choice voting (RCV)," Ballotpedia, accessed July 14, 2021, https://ballotpedia.org/Ranked-choice_voting_(RCV).

108   Leonie Huddy, Lilliana Mason, and Lene Aarøe, "Expressive Partisanship: Campaign Involvement, Political Emotion, and Partisan Identity," The American Political Science Review 109, no. 1 (2015): 1–17.

109   Miller and Conover, "Red and Blue States of Mind," 225–239.

Chapter 7

110   Charles E. Canady, *Running To Win: A Step-by-Step Campaign Guide* (Lakeland: Morris/Jeffries Publishing, 1999).

111   Canady, *Running To Win*.

112   Ron Faucheux, eds., *The Road to Victory: The Complete Guide to Winning Political Campaigns – Local, State and Federal*, 2nd ed. (Dubuque, IA: Kendall/Hunt Publishing Company, 1998).

113   "Access To and Use of Voter Registration Lists," National Conference of State Legislatures (website), accessed July 14, 2021, https://www.ncsl.org/research/elections-and-campaigns/access-to-and-use-of-voter-registration-lists.aspx.

114   Drew DeSilver, "In past elections, U.S. trailed most developed countries in voter turnout," Pew Research Center, November 3, 2020, https://www.pewresearch.org/fact-tank/2020/11/03/in-past-elections-u-s-trailed-most-developed-countries-in-voter-turnout/.

115   Huddy, Mason, and Aarøe, "Expressive Partisanship," 1–17.

116   Miller and Conover, "Red and Blue States of Mind," 225–239.

117   Huddy, Mason, and Aarøe, "Expressive Partisanship," 1–17.

118   Miller and Conover, "Red and Blue States of Mind," 225–239.

119   "About Us," Unite America, accessed June 22, 2021, https://www.uniteamerica.org/about.

120   "Partners," Unite America, accessed June 21, 2021, https://www.uniteamerica.org/partners.

Chapter 8

121   "Ballot access requirements for political candidates in Indiana," Ballotpedia, accessed June 21, 2021, https:// ballotpedia.org/Ballot_access_requirements_for_political_candidates_in_Indiana.

122   "Ballot access requirements for political candidates in Texas," Ballotpedia, accessed June 21, 2021, https:// ballotpedia.org/Ballot_access_requirements_for_political_candidates_in_Texas.

123   "Republican or Democratic Party Nominees," Texas Secretary of State, accessed June 21, 2021, https://www.sos.state.tx.us/elections/candidates/guide/2018/demorrep2018.shtml.

124   "Independent Candidates," Texas Secretary of State, https://www.sos.state.tx.us/elections/candidates/guide/2018/ind2018.shtml.

125   "Race Summary Report 2014 General Election," Texas Secretary of State, accessed June 21, 2021, https://elections.sos.state.tx.us/elchist175_state.htm.

126   "Indiana Code 2020 3-8-2-8," Indiana General Assembly (website), accessed June 21, 2021, http://iga.in.gov/legislative/laws/2020/ic/titles/003#3-8-2-8.

127   "Indiana Code 2020 3-8-6-3."

128   "List of political parties of the United States," Ballotpedia, accessed June 21, 2021, https://ballotpedia.org/List_of_political_parties_in_the_United_States.

129   "Information about Recognized Political Parties," Arizona Secretary of State, accessed June 21, 2021, https:// azsos.gov/elections/information-about-recognized-political-parties.

130   "Political Groups," Alaska Division of Elections,

accessed July 24, 2021, https://www.elections.alaska.gov/Core/politicalgroups.php.

131   James L. Baumgardner, "The 1888 Presidential Election: How Corrupt?" *Presidential Studies Quarterly* 14, no. 3 (1984) 416–427.

132   "Evan McMullin," Ballotpedia, accessed June 21, 2021, https://ballotpedia.org/Evan_McMullin.

133   "Fact check: Are the presidential debates rigged in favor of major party candidates?" Ballotpedia, accessed July 10, 2021, https://ballotpedia.org/Fact_check/Are_the_presidential_debates_rigged_in_favor_of_major_party_candidates.

134   "The First Televised Presidential Debate," United States Senate, accessed June 21, 2021, https://www.senate.gov/artandhistory/history/minute/The_First_Televised_Presidential_Debate.htm.

Chapter 9

135   "Presidential debates (2015–2016)," Ballotpedia, accessed July 14, 2021, https://ballotpedia.org/Presidential_debates_(2015-2016).

136   "Gary Johnson presidential campaign 2016," Ballotpedia, accessed July 14, 2021, https://ballotpedia.org/Gary_Johnson_presidential_campaign,_2016.

137   "CNN/ORC International Poll," WarnerMedia, accessed July 14, 2021, http://i2.cdn.turner.com/cnn/2016/images/07/17/rel8a.-.2016.pdf.

138   "General Election: Trump vs. Clinton vs. Johnson vs. Stein (2-Way Race)," RealClearPolitics, accessed July 14, 2021, https://www.realclearpolitics.com/epolls/2016/president/us/general_election_trump_vs_clinton_vs_john-

son_vs_stein-5952.html.

139   "2016," The American Presidency Project, accessed July 14, 2021, https://www.presidency.ucsb.edu/statistics/elections/2016.

140   Elaine C. Kamarck and Ashley Gabriele, Brookings Institution (website), accessed July 14, 2021, https://www.brookings.edu/wp-content/uploads/2016/07/new-media.pdf.

141   Elizabeth Grieco, "10 charts about America's newsrooms," Pew Research Center, April 28, 2020, https://www.pewresearch.org/fact-tank/2020/04/28/10-charts-about-americas-newsrooms/.

142   "The news today: 7 trends in old and new media."

143   Amy Mitchell, Jeffrey Gottfried, Jocelyn Kiley, and Katerina Eva Matsa, "Political Polarization & Media Habits," Pew Research Center, October 21, 2014, https://www.journalism.org/2014/10/21/political-polarization-media-habits/.

144   Ronald Brownstein, *The Second Civil War: How Extreme Partisanship Has Paralyzed Washington and Polarized America* (New York: Penguin Group, 2007).

145   E.E. Schattschneider, *The Semisovereign People: A Realist's View of Democracy in America* (New York: Holt, Rinehart, and Winston, 1960).

146   Stephen C. Craig and David B. Hill, eds., *The Electoral Challenge: Theory Meets Practice*, 2nd ed. (Washington, DC: CQ Press, 2011) 144-161.

147   Miller and Wattenberg, "Measuring Party Identification," 106–121.

148   Harry Enten, "Fake Polls Are A Real Problem," *FiveThirtyEight*, August 22, 2017, https://fivethirtyeight.com/features/fake-polls-are-a-real-problem/.

149   Blais, André, et al. "Do Polls Influence the Vote?" Capturing Campaign Effects, edited by Henry E. Brady and Richard Johnston (Ann Arbor, Michigan: University of Michigan Press, 2006) 263–279.

150   John C. Blydenburgh, "Sophisticated Voting in the 1980 Presidential Election," *Political Behavior* 10, no. 2 (1988): 103–116.

151   Larry M. Bartels, "Expectations and Preferences in Presidential Nominating Campaigns," *The American Political Science Review* 79, no. 3 (1985): 804–815.

152   Richard L. Henshel and William Johnston, "The Emergence of Bandwagon Effects: A Theory," *The Sociological Quarterly* 28, no. 4 (1987): 493–511.

153   David J. Lanoue and Shaun Bowler, "Picking the Winners: Perceptions of Party Viability and Their Impact on Voting Behavior," *Social Science Quarterly* 79, no. 2 (1998): 361–377.

Chapter 10

154   Paul A. Beck, "Encouraging Political Defection: The Role of Personal Discussion Networks in Partisan Desertions to the Opposition Party and Perot Votes in 1992," *Political Behavior* 24, no. 4 (2002): 309–377.

155   "Elected Officials," Libertarian Party, accessed August 11, 2021, https://my.lp.org/elected-officials/.

156   "Summary of Green Candidates 2019," GPUS Elections Database, accessed July 14, 2021, https://www.gpelections.org/?t=2019.

157   "Summary of Green Candidates 2020," GPUS Elections Database, accessed July 14, 2021, https://www.gpelections.org/?t=2020.

158 "Maine gubernatorial election, 2010."

159 "Current independent and third-party federal and state officeholders," Ballotpedia, accessed June 16, 2021, https://ballotpedia.org/Current_independent_and_third-party_federal_and_state_officeholders.

160 Kenneth Mulligan, "Partisan Ambivalence, Split-Ticket Voting, and Divided Government," *Political Psychology* 32, no. 3 (2011): 505–530.

161 "Bullock v. Carter," Ballotpedia, accessed July 14, 2021, https://ballotpedia.org/Bullock_v._Carter.

162 "Bullock v. Carter," Oyez (website), accessed July 14, 2021, https://www.oyez.org/cases/1971/70-128.

163 "Lubin v. Panish," Ballotpedia, accessed July 14, 2021, https://ballotpedia.org/Lubin_v._Panish.

164 "Lubin v. Panish, 415 U.S. 709 (1974)," Justia US Supreme Court Center, accessed July 14, 2021, https://supreme.justia.com/cases/federal/us/415/709/.

165 "Storer v. Brown," Ballotpedia, accessed July 14, 2021, https://ballotpedia.org/Storer_v._Brown.

166 "Storer v. Brown, 415 U.S. 724 (1974)," Justia US Supreme Court Center, accessed July 14, 2021, https://supreme.justia.com/cases/federal/us/415/724/.

167 "Illinois State Board of Elections v. Socialist Workers Party," Ballotpedia, accessed July 14, 2021, https://ballotpedia.org/Illinois_State_Board_of_Elections_v._Socialist_Workers_Party.

168 "Illinois State Bd. of Elections v. Socialist Workers Party, 440 U.S. 173 (1979)," Justia US Supreme Court Center, accessed July 14, 2021, https://supreme.justia.com/cases/federal/us/440/173/.

169 "Ballot access for major and minor party candidates," Ballotpedia, accessed July 14, 2021, https://ballotpe-

dia.org/Ballot_access_for_major_and_minor_party_candidates.

170   "Anderson v. Celebrezze," Ballotpedia, accessed July 14, 2021, https://ballotpedia.org/Anderson_v._Celebrezze.

171   "Anderson v. Celebrezze, 460 U.S. 780 (1983)," Justia US Supreme Court Center, accessed July 14, 2021, https://supreme.justia.com/cases/federal/us/460/780/.

172   "Norman v. Reed," Ballotpedia, accessed July 14, 2021, https://ballotpedia.org/Norman_v._Reed.

173   "Norman v. Reed (1992)," *The Free Speech Center – Middle Tennessee State University*, accessed July 14, 2021, https://www.mtsu.edu/first-amendment/article/148/norman-v-reed.

Chapter 11

174   Stephen C. Craig, James G. Kane, and Michael D. Martinez, "Sometimes You Feel like a Nut, Sometimes You Don't: Citizens' Ambivalence about Abortion," *Political Psychology* 23, no. 2 (2002): 285–301.

175   Dmitri Evseev, "A Second Look at Third Parties: Correcting the Supreme Court's Understanding of Elections," *Boston University Law Review* 85 (2005): 1277–1331.

176   "Our Strategy," Unite America (website), accessed July 14, 2021, https://www.uniteamerica.org/strategy.

177   "Redistricting," Ballotpedia, accessed June 23, 2021, https://ballotpedia.org/Redistricting.

178   "Redistricting commissions," Ballotpedia, accessed June 23, 2021, https://ballotpedia.org/Redistricting_commissions.

179   Bonneau and Cann, "Party Identification and Vote Choice," 43–66.

180   "Nebraska State Senate partisan affiliation."

181   "All-mail voting," Ballotpedia, accessed June 23, 2021, https://ballotpedia.org/All-mail_voting.

182   "Vote at Home," Unite America (website), accessed July 14, 2021, https://www.uniteamerica.org/strategy/vote-at-home.

183   "Colorado Voting Reforms: Early Results," The Pew Charitable Trusts, March 22, 2016, https://www.pewtrusts.org/en/research-and-analysis/issue-briefs/2016/03/colorado-voting-reforms-early-results.

184   Adam J. Berinsky, "The Perverse Consequences of Electoral Reform in the United States," *American Politics Research* 33, no. 4 (2005): 471–91.

185   "Vote at Home."

186   Beck, "Encouraging Political Defection," 309–377.

187   Bill Allison, Mira Rojanasakul, Brittany Harris, and Cedric Sam, "Tracking the 2016 Presidential Money Race," Bloomberg News, December 9, 2016, https://www.bloomberg.com/politics/graphics/2016-presidential-campaign-fundraising/.

188   Earl Latham, "The Group Basis of Politics: Notes for a Theory," *The American Political Science Review* 46, no. 2 (1952): 376–97.

189   Olson, *The Logic of Collective Action*.

190   John H. Aldrich, *Why Parties? A Second Look* (Chicago: The University of Chicago Press, 2011) 27-64.

191   "Home," SAM – A New Party for a New Majority (website), accessed July 14, 2021, https://joinsam.org/.

192   Matthew Levendusky and Neil Malhotra, "Does Media Coverage of Partisan Polarization Affect Political Attitudes?" *Political Communication* 33, no. 2 (2016): 283–301.

193   Matthew S. Levendusky, "Why Do Partisan Media Polarize Voters?" *American Journal of Political Science* 57, no. 3 (2013): 611–623.

194   Matthew S. Levendusky and Neil Malhotra, "(Mis) perceptions of Partisan Polarization in the American Public," *Public Opinion Quarterly* 80, no. S1 (2015): 378–391.

195   Douglas J. Ahler, "Self-Fulfilling Misperceptions of Public Polarization," *The Journal of Politics* 76, no. 3 (2014): 607–620.

196   Ahler, "Self-Fulfilling Misperceptions," 607–620.

197   Philip M. Fernbach, Todd Rogers, Craig R. Fox, and Steven A. Sloman, "Political Extremism is Supported by an Illusion of Understanding," *Psychological Science* 24, no. 6 (2013): 939–946.

198   Fiorina, Abrams, and Pope, "Polarization in the American Public," 556–560.

199   "Political Typology Reveals Deep Fissures on the Right and Left."

Made in United States
Orlando, FL
16 September 2023

37009790R00124